D1381836

The Bible

Faith and the Future
General Editor: David Nicholls

Choices
Ethics and the Christian
David Brown

Church and Nation
Peter Cornwell

Pastoral Care and the Parish
Peter Davie

The Faith Abroad
John D. Davies

Church, Ministry and Unity
A Divine Commission
James E. Griffiss

The Authority of Divine Love
Richard Harries

The Bible
Fountain and Well of Truth
John Muddiman

Faith, Prayer and Devotion
Ralph Townsend

Sacraments and Liturgy
The Outward Signs
Louis Weil

The Bible

*Fountain and
Well of Truth*

John Muddiman

Basil Blackwell

© John Muddiman 1983

First published 1983
Reprinted 1985

Basil Blackwell Publisher Limited
108 Cowley Road, Oxford OX4 1JF, UK

Basil Blackwell Inc.
432 Park Avenue South, Suite 1505,
New York, NY 10016, USA

British Library Cataloguing in Publication Data
Muddiman, John
    The Bible: fountain and well of truth.
    1. Bible — Criticism and interpretation, etc
    I. Title
    220.6   BS511.2

    ISBN 0-631-13188-4
    ISBN 0-631-13231-7 Pbk

Typeset by Cambrian Typesetters
Farnborough, Hants
Printed in Great Britain
by T. J. Press Ltd, Padstow

Contents

Foreword *by Bishop Michael Ramsey*   vii

1 Christian Faith and Biblical Criticism   1

2 Images of Hope: the Old Testament   20

3 The Word Incarnate: Jesus and the Gospels   38

4 Believing in the Body of Christ: Paul and
   the New Testament Canon   67

5 A Biblical Agenda   88

General Reading   104

Notes   106

Index of Biblical References   112

Index of Names and Subjects   114

Foreword

This book is one of a series whose writers consider some important aspects of Christianity in the contemporary scene and in so doing draw inspiration from the Catholic revival in the Anglican Communion which began in Oxford one hundred and fifty years ago. This revival — with its thinkers, pastors, prophets, social reformers and not a few who have been held to be saints — has experienced changes in the understanding of the Christian faith since the time of the Tractarians and has none the less borne witness to themes which are deep and unchanging. Among these are the call to holiness, the communion of saints, the priesthood of the Church and its ministers and a sacramental religion, both otherworldly and with revolutionary claims upon man's social life.

I am myself convinced that the renewal of the Church for today and tomorrow needs a deep recovery of these themes of Catholic tradition and a vision of their contemporary application. The books of this series are designed towards this end, and I am sure that readers will be grateful for the help they give. Many are thirsty but 'the well is deep'.

✠ Michael Ramsey

1 Christian Faith and Biblical Criticism

THE FOUNTAIN AND THE WELL

This is a book about the Bible in the Church. It is not intended as an introduction to biblical study, or a popular survey of scholarship, or a spiritual meditation on biblical themes. Very good books on all these subjects already exist.[1] It is rather an attempt to discuss a difficult and urgent problem which is commonly referred to nowadays as the 'use and abuse of the Bible'.[2] Biblical criticism accuses the Church of misusing the Bible. Christian believers feel that criticism, instead of really *using* the Bible, is just being abusive about it. How, then, is the Bible to be used by the Church?

Scripture has regained a position of remarkable prominence in the life of the Church in the twentieth century. It provides the common language of ecumenical dialogue, spoken as fluently by Roman Catholics as by other Christians. It is regularly re-issued in lively modern translations, and the liturgy has been rewritten in the new biblical idiom. The old, chaotic lectionaries have been abandoned in favour of sets of little passages on selected themes, and the Christian at prayer is encouraged to use the Bible, and given every possible assistance in notes and guides. But the net result of this renewed prominence of scripture is often increased confusion. We understand more of the words but less of the meaning. The lofty, oracular quality of the old use of the Bible, which gave it a vague kind of stylistic unity, has been lost, and the oddity and diversity of the views expressed in the Bible now appear in stark relief. Once Christians venture beyond the passages

1

prescribed for their spiritual diet in the liturgy, they begin to feel out of their depth, lost in the detail and occasionally even alienated from it all. So the use and meaning of the Bible, in its different parts and as a whole, is an issue of acute concern for the Church today.

In 1543 Archbishop Thomas Cranmer wrote a sermon entitled *A Fruitful Exhortation to the Reading of Holy Scripture*, which was published four years later in the first *Book of Homilies*.[3] When ministers of the English Church are stuck for a sermon, they are authorized to read one of these official homilies instead, though, not unwisely, they seldom do. However, Cranmer's description there of the Bible as 'the fountain and the well of truth' may serve as a text and summary of the approach I intend to take to the problem. The Bible is like a well, deep and inaccessible, from which truth has to be extracted laboriously by study through the method of biblical criticism. But the Bible is also like a fountain, fresh and accessible, with its own power to communicate truth to the receptive mind; let us call this 'the method of faith'. I propose to consider the Bible in its two aspects as fountain and well, and to explore the interaction between the method of criticism and the method of faith.

The critical method starts from the principle that no special privileges attach to the Bible as a text for study. The biblical literature is placed on the same level as other ancient writings of a similar kind, and allowed to establish itself 'from below' by its own merits, not by preferential treatment. Criticism focuses attention chiefly on what the individual books meant when they were written. When it moves away from this, it is usually in the direction of the prehistory of the text, the origin of the ideas the authors use, or the reconstruction of the historical facts which they purport to relate. It is satisfied when it has given as complete an explanation as possible of the book as it was written, or has successfully run its ideas or its facts to ground.

When I distinguish faith from criticism, I do not mean that where the critical method is rigorous and sceptical,

2

faith is unquestioning and gullible. I referred above to the *method* of faith, precisely to avoid that misconception. The difference has rather to do with the starting point from which faith approaches the Bible, and the goal towards which it aims. For faith, the Bible has a privileged position, represented by the canon of scripture and the liturgical practice of the Church. It is interested in what the individual books mean in relation to the whole of scripture, and what they mean for belief in God today. The method of faith is satisfied only when it has given as complete an account as possible of the totality of scripture and of its own encounter with God in Christ.

The Church cannot afford to neglect either of these methods in its search for the truth. Faith without criticism would detach the Church from the reality of the world. What might appear at first as a cosy option turns out to be a dangerously exposed position. If the believing community lacks the courage to be critical of itself, which includes examining the accuracy and plausibility of its historical claims and the original meaning of the Bible, there is no shortage of daring assailants from outside eager to do the job for it. And the Church's acceptance of criticism should not be merely a grudging concession for the sake of better apologetics. If it is really truth that faith discloses, then faith should embrace criticism for the sake of truth. The hard realities of the world in which the critical method deals are the very same hard realities which faith identifies as the creation of God.

On the other hand, criticism without faith detaches the Church from the Spirit. It falsifies the totality of the truth by dividing it up for analysis. A fountain is not just so many bucketfuls of water. And the Bible approached by the method of faith is an open system, like a fountain, whose shape is determined by the free flow of energy through it. It is only within the believing community, where the energy of the Spirit gives form to the tradition, that scripture as a whole can be truly interpreted and received.

The fountain and the well are themselves biblical images,

and we may pause at this point and listen to them speak. The people of Israel always remembered their origins in the desert; and when the wandering tribes came to rest in Canaan they were reminded of their past by the haunting symbol of the wilderness of Judaea. Their yearning for God felt like a thirst for water in a dry land. They longed for 'the fountain of life', as the Psalmist put it, or 'the wells of salvation' in Isaiah's phrase. Paradise lost, for them, was a garden amply irrigated by running streams, and the new Temple of Ezekiel has rivers flowing from beneath its threshold. The new Jerusalem will be a garden city, paradise regained. The prophetic summons to return to God, and Wisdom's gentle appeal to live in accordance with his reasonable laws, are expressed in the form of the command to 'come and drink'. The insatiable thirst for God and the aridity of ordinary existence: these biblical images come together and achieve a certain fulfilment in a passage from the gospel according to John. The dialogue between Jesus and the Samaritan woman represents the wearisome reality of life in the world symbolically in the need to draw water from a well, and yet points towards faith in Christ as a flowing fountain, sufficient to satisfy our thirst for God. The passage reads:

Jesus had to pass through Samaria, and in doing so he arrived at a Samaritan town called Sychar; it lay near the territory which Jacob had given to his son Joseph, and 'Jacob's Spring' was there. Jesus, exhausted by the journey, sat down at the spring, just as he was. It was about noon. And a Samaritan woman come to draw water. Jesus said to her, 'Give me a drink.' The Samaritan woman said, 'What? You are a Jew, and you ask me for a drink — me, a Samaritan!' Jesus answered, 'If you knew what is the free gift of God and who is asking you for a drink, you would have asked him instead, and he would have given you "living" water.' 'Sir,' said the woman, 'you have nothing to draw water with, and it is a deep well; where do you get your "living" water? Are you a greater man than Jacob, our ancestor? He gave us this well, and he drank from it, with his sons and his cattle.' Jesus answered, 'Anyone who drinks this water will be thirsty again, but anyone who drinks the water I shall give him will never thirst any more; the water I shall give him will turn into a spring of water welling up to eternal life.' 'Ah, sir,' said the woman, 'give me this water, so that I need not thirst or come all this road to draw water.'[4]

This woman, for reasons which are only brought to light later in the dialogue, is trying to avoid human company. She does not use the water supply in the village, but comes out to this lonely spot in the heat of the day, when no-one else is likely to be about. And she carries with her a bucket and the necessary length of rope. The stranger, evidently a Jew from his distinctive dress, is sitting on the stone that covers the mouth of the well to stop careless animals falling in and poisoning it. So she cannot avoid him, and he confronts her first by asking for a drink. Her defensive reply masks the deeper reason for her hesitation, but already Jesus reads her thoughts and says: 'If you knew what God can give — water to drink and to wash away your sin — and if you knew the identity of the one whom God has sent to perform this cleansing and this refreshment, the roles would have been reversed. You would have asked him, and he would have supplied the running water.' Understanding only the superficial meaning of his words, she is intrigued by the idea of getting fresh water from a deep well without the aid of a rope. A trick worthy of Jacob himself!

The patriarch Jacob, the last common ancestor before the division of Israel into tribes, was a hero of the Samaritans, and he appears to have had a way with wells. In Genesis 29, we are told that he was sent to find a wife from among his own kin, and came across a well covered by a large stone, surrounded by flocks of sheep bleating noisily to be watered. It was midday on that occasion too, and he saw in the distance the figure of a woman, Rachel his cousin and his future bride. To save her a long wait in the heat, Jacob himself removed the stone from the well and drew the water. And he was willing to spend seven and even fourteen years drawing water, to gain her hand in marriage; the time 'seemed to him but a few days because of the love he had for her'.

Later tradition embroidered this story with a pretty legend. Divine mercy, it conjectured, must have relieved the labours of Jacob by working a miracle that made it easier for him to endure the delay: 'After our ancestor Jacob had lifted the stone from the mouth of the well, the water rose to its surface and overflowed and was overflowing twenty years.'[5] And now, at last, in the gospel story, a greater than Jacob is here and a lesser than Rachel is here along with him. Under his influence, the well becomes a fountain springing up to eternal life. The living water he gives refreshes the thirsty soul, and washes every sin away. At the beginning of the story we had been told that this was 'Jacob's Spring', but the woman has consistently referred to it as a well. The life has gone out of the old story. But it is a function of the new Jacob to turn the well back into a spring by his reviving presence.

This is the analogy we are using[6] for the interaction of criticism and faith. We can approach the Bible as a well, hidden and distanced from us, a collection of writings produced over the space of a millennium, from 900 BC to AD 100, containing the theology and poetry, history and ethics of the people of Israel and their spiritual heirs. This approach requires the effort and patience of critical research. It needs a bucket and a long rope, a method for extracting the truth from the depths of the past. But the critical method has its risks: the bucket may leak or get snagged or spill on the way up; the rope may fray and snap; the sheer weight may be too much for unaided human effort to bring to the surface. The advantage of the method is that it produces a reasonably predictable supply, and can be refined and improved upon over the years, and the patient and industrious drawer of water may yet manage to slake his own thirst and that of many others.

But scripture is also a fountain of truth. Mysteriously in the presence of the living Christ, the truth behind the text can rise to the surface of its own accord, and be apprehended in all its freshness and immediacy. The Bible has this mysterious or 'sacramental' quality; it can become the vehicle of communication with the Spirit of God. Ordinary Bible readers may themselves be uncritical and misinformed, but their deficiencies, like the unworthiness of the priest at the altar, do not hinder the effect of grace. Their experience authenticates itself within the believing community. It does not, of course, authenticate anything else. It cannot validate historical or logical errors, and each individual believer has to submit his or her own perception of it to the test of the same experience in others. But it is this experience of encounter with the Spirit through the reading of scripture, the method of faith practised in the community of faith, which the Church has tried to articulate by speaking of the Bible as *infallible* and *inspired*. Biblical critics are understandably wary of such language, for fear that their hands are being tied and that their freedom to follow their course wherever it leads is being restricted. But the certainty of faith and the freedom of critical enquiry are not necessarily opposites, if both are harnessed to the search for the truth.

In the remaining sections of this chapter, I shall try to argue that unhindered biblical criticism and the continuous tradition of Christian faith need each other, if the truth of scripture is to become available to the Church today.

FAITH AND TRADITION

When we say that the meaning of scripture can be apprehended by faith with a kind of mysterious immediacy, we are quite likely to be misunderstood, unless we define the matter further. It may be possible sometimes for an individual Christian to perceive the truth of a particular passage of the Bible through the exercise of private intuition, or, as he or she may prefer to express it, through the influence of the Holy Spirit. But this is not the primary sense in which

I am using the metaphor of the Bible as the fountain of truth. The channel through which faith approaches the Bible is not individual but corporate. No single believer possesses the totality of the Holy Spirit in such a way that his or her reading of scripture carries the guarantee of right interpretation. On the contrary, the Holy Spirit is precisely the way theology chooses to speak of the limitations placed on human individuality. The Spirit is the corporate activity of God, creating unity and conviction out of a wide variety of gifts and insights (see 1 Corinthians 12: 4—11). In other words, the fountain to which I am referring is the Church's living tradition of faith.

Tradition may occasionally become crystallized or even temporarily frozen in the creeds or definitions of councils, in authorized liturgical texts or the instructions of church leaders, but it is essentially a dynamic principle, the handing on and celebration of a lively faith in God through Christ. When it is understood like this, tradition can never be set in opposition to scripture, as it has sometimes been.[7] Tradition is both the ground from which Christian scripture once grew, and also the process by which the meaning of the Bible is constantly reappropriated by the believing community. Failure in the past to recognize the integrity of scripture and tradition was perhaps the major cause of divisions between Christians, and our growing awareness today of their interdependence is a sign of hope for the future reintegration of the Church.

In primitive Christianity it is impossible to distinguish scripture and tradition as separate sources of truth. The early Church was slow to produce written statements of what it knew of Christ, for the belief in the imminence of his return in glory seemed to make them unnecessary. Even when they did appear, more time was to elapse before such writings attained the status of Christian scripture. The Old Testament alone was the Church's Bible until well into the second century AD. Christianity therefore began as tradition in two senses of the word.

First, there was the oral tradition of the good news of Christ. This was conveyed in the community's memory of Jesus' words and deeds, and especially of his Passion, and was formulated in preaching and liturgy. It also contained summaries of the significance of the work of Christ, like that handed on to the Corinthians by Paul:

> I delivered to you as of first importance what I also received, that Christ died for our sins in accordance with the scripture, that he was buried, that he was raised on the third day in accordance with the scriptures, and that he appeared . . . (1 Corinthians 15: 3–4).

This preference for oral tradition endured into the age of the Apostolic Fathers. As Ignatius of Antioch (died c. AD 110) says: 'It is Jesus Christ who is the original documents: the inviolable archives are his cross and death and resurrection, and the faith that came by him.'[8]

Second, Christianity began as a tradition of interpreting Old Testament scripture in the light of its fulfilment in the coming of the Messiah. The scribal tradition of scriptural interpretation had been rejected by Jesus (Mark 7:8) but he had supported that rejection by himself offering an interpretation of the prophecy of Isaiah (29:13): 'They worship me in vain, teaching as doctrines the precepts of men.' What Jesus advocated, then, was not acceptance of the words of the Old Testament simply in their original sense without any attempt to explain their meaning for the present time of fulfilment, but rather a proper, that is not evasive or hypocritical, interpretation of scripture. As St Paul says in 2 Corinthians 3:17f, when we turn to Christ in the freedom of the Spirit, the veil of obscurity that hangs over the text of scripture is removed, and the glory of God's self-unveiling in Christ shines with ever-increasing clarity.

When, at the Council of Nicaea in AD 325, a list or 'canon' of New Testament writings was finally authorized, this was not a victory for scripture over tradition, or for tradition (in this instance the authority of a council) over scripture. For the bishops at Nicaea were at one and the same time acknowledging the supremacy of scripture and setting up tradition as the key to the proper understanding of it. They recognized the evident authority of the Christian literature which had found acceptance in liturgical use by the Church; but they also provided by means of the canon itself a framework of interpretation for the writings that were included. For scripture was to be read as a whole: the Old Testament as fulfilled in the New; the letters of Paul in full, and in conjunction with the Acts of the Apostles and other letters; John's gospel to be read with the other three, not against them, and so forth. Thus, the principle of the supreme authority of scripture for Christian faith does not at all imply disrespect for tradition. The fixed canon of scripture was intended to exclude not tradition, but non-scriptural writings (especially heretical works) and perverse (that is untraditional) interpretations of scripture.

When the Reformers of the sixteenth century affirmed that scripture contained all things necessary to salvation, they were not intending to set the Bible in opposition to tradition in the senses discussed above. They were rather challenging false interpretations and unscriptural additions to traditional faith. It was, at least at first, an attempt to distinguish between 'good, old tradition', in Martin Luther's phrase, and recent, corrupt innovation. Some reformers took the principle to imply that only that which could be explicitly proved from scripture was to be retained, but others, including most English Reformers, argued that only what was explicitly rejected by scripture had to be abandoned.

The Roman Catholic response at the Council of Trent (1546) was to claim scripture and tradition as equal sources of revelation to be 'treated with the same love and respect'.[9] Within the larger concept of tradition, the Council discerned several forms. It recognized that at many points tradition coincides with scripture, or gives the true sense of an obscure passage of the Bible. Both of these forms of tradition the Reformers accepted, although they called them scripture and not tradition! But Trent also allowed for what is called 'constitutive tradition', where tradition goes beyond scripture. This was and still is a major point of conflict between the Roman Catholic and Protestant churches. It concerns such matters as the cult of the saints, papal infallibility and the doctrinal implications of devotion to Mary. There is, however, some indication that modern Catholic theologians, while holding to the truth of their church's teaching on these questions, are willing to see doctrines which are based solely on constitutive tradition as relatively less important and lower down, as it were, in the hierarchy of truths than doctrines which have a scriptural basis.

In the debates following the Reformation period, a deep divide seemed to open up between the sides on the problem of scripture and tradition. Protestantism began to lapse into a narrow biblicism, and break up into smaller sects over minor differences of scriptural exegesis. Catholicism by reaction appeared to adopt a hard and arrogant traditionalism. In the modern period, however, we have seen a remarkable change in the climate of the debate, illustrated by the documents of two international conferences: the World Council of Churches Faith and Order conference at Montreal in 1963 and the Second Vatican Council (1962–64).

The churches represented at Montreal abandoned the false opposition of scripture and tradition and proposed a new distinction between common Christian Tradition and the traditions of the separated churches. By Tradition was meant 'The Gospel itself, transmitted from generation to generation in and by the Church, Christ himself present in the life of the Church.'[10] Scripture is, then, not to be understood as over against the living tradition of the Church but as bearing written testimony to it. And scripture has to be reinterpreted by the Church in ever new situations, for the mere reiteration of the words of holy scripture would be a betrayal of the requirement that the Gospel must be made intelligible and challenging to men and women today. Montreal looked to the encounter of the churches in the ecumenical movement and critical study of the Bible by scholars of the different denominations in

11

co-operation, as the means of discerning true Tradition and thereby purifying the various confessional traditions of whatever errors still separate them.

In the same eirenic spirit, the Second Vatican Council replaced polemical references to 'constitutive' tradition of the Council of Trent with an integrated view. The Dogmatic Constitution on Divine Revelation stated that there is 'a close connection and communication between sacred tradition and sacred Scripture. For both of them, flowing from the same divine wellspring, in a certain way merge into a unity and tend towards the same end'.[11] Such a view opens up the possibility for the Roman Catholic Church to develop a degree of self-criticism towards those traditions of its own which breach this unity of scripture and tradition, and this is the direction which, by and large, it has continued to follow.

THE INEVITABILITY OF CRITICISM

Now that Catholics and Protestants in ecumenical dialogue have declared an armistice over scripture and tradition, and indeed appear to be competing with each other to justify the correctness of the view of the other side, it is noticeable that biblical critics are finding themselves more isolated. Once in the forefront of ecumenism, some have cooled in their enthusiasm, fearing perhaps that inter-denominational courtesies may blunt the edge of scholarship and domesticate it to the service of ecclesiastical harmony. Whereas before they used to emphasize the unity of scripture over against the divergent tendencies of later church traditions, they have recently begun to point out the diversity of views within the Bible. It is important therefore to insist at this point that critical study of scripture is not an optional extra to faith, which can be employed so long as it is convenient and helpful but otherwise ignored. On the contrary, it is the Bible itself which makes criticism inevitable and defends its freedom in practice.

In the first place, it is the very form of scripture which necessitates criticism. The Bible is not a corpus of doctrinal propositions requiring simply to be expounded and applied.[12] The largest part of it is cast in narrative form, but a narrative which is neither a record of fact free of interpretation, nor a complex of authoritative and theological opinions disguised as history. Criticism is needed if these narrative portions of scripture are to be properly appreciated as 'interpreted history', and not as plain event or unalterable theory. The critic tells us what the facts are likely to have been to which the writer was reacting and why he reacted in the way he did; the way is thus opened for the Christian reader to re-use the narrative in the believing community. The critical process of thinking one's way back to the situation of the original author is made inevitable by the narrative form of presentation, which invites sympathetic participation from the reader. But neither the critic nor the believer is content simply to take over the biblical author's interpretation as the last word; they each reserve the right to relive the experience, so to speak, for themselves in the present. When the liturgy of the Easter Vigil joins together the deliverance of Israel from bondage in Egypt and the resurrection of Jesus 'on this night in which heaven is wedded to earth', there is also at the same time a marriage of criticism and faith. For the believer knows and the critic demonstrates historically that the meaning of Exodus and the Resurrection is not exhausted by the description of them as past events; to be understood properly they must also be seen as paradigms of salvation.

Much of the Bible is written in the form of poetry, more indeed than is often apparent from the way the text is printed: the Psalms, the prophetic oracles, the wisdom literature, much of the teaching of Jesus, and even the hymns of Paul like 'the Ode to Love' in 1 Corinthians 13. Here again the basic form of scripture requires both criticism, in the sense of literary appreciation, and also faith, in the sense of active participation of the reader in the creation of meaning. For poetry is a way of expressing truth equivocally, in hints that demand the exercise of the reader's imagination. Similarly, the biblical material which

13

is cast in the form of law has no meaning in isolation from the interpretative activity of a judge who will apply the rules to actual instances in all their contingent complexity and test them against the principle of consistency in judgement. Whether the laws are ramified into a system of casuistry as in orthodox Judaism, or condensed into the spirit and new law of Christ, they by reason of their form make criticism and a tradition of interpretation inevitable.

The historical-critical method, as it has been refined over the last 150 years, is necessary for other reasons also.[13] The authority of the Bible is not first questioned by criticism. It is already questionable because of the striking inconsistencies in the text; and the critical solutions to these inconsistencies have the effect of restoring value to scripture. The source criticism of the Pentateuch, for instance, provides the only satisfactory answer to conflicts over the revelation of the Divine Name[14] and many similar anachronisms. The study of the prehistory of the text not only uncovers the internal coherence of the individual pieces of the mosaic, so to speak, but it actually re-establishes its authority in that sense of the word 'authority' which alone is likely to find ready acceptance with us today. For it points us towards the community that preserved and eventually assembled these traditions. And for us also, the authority of authors comes a poor second to the authority of communities, the authority of consensus related to our accumulated and shared experience in society.

In many passages of scripture, it is worth remembering, the alternative to the critical reading is not the simple sense of it, but the patent nonsense of it from our perspective. The critical explanation may emphasize its strangeness and pastness, its 'irrelevance' as we say, to our present situation, but its 'irrelevance' is itself relevant, if it reminds us that our search for truth is bound to take us out of ourselves and our own concerns.

The critique of the historical veracity of the Bible is perhaps what the ordinary believer finds most disconcerting in the critical method. Certain critics have, admittedly, given just cause for alarm; they have sometimes allowed philosophical prejudice to lead them into betraying their own method by becoming hypercritical, and subjecting the Bible to tests of reliability which no historical document could ever pass. But in principle there is nothing unscriptural about the critical method. The history of Israel is a story told 'warts and all'; the sins of the people are scarlet on every page of the Old Testament; the betrayal of Jesus by his own disciples and the bitter controversies of the early Church are not concealed or papered over. If, then, the critic exposes to criticism the remaining vestiges of the human impulse to glorify ourselves in our own history, to exaggerate, for example, the scale of the victories in the book of Joshua or the orderliness of missionary expansion in the Acts of the Apostles, he may well claim to be acting in accordance with the spirit of scripture as a whole.

Even when criticism does not positively demonstrate that a biblical writer is guilty of human fallibility and bias, it can unnerve the believer by its uncertainty and inconclusiveness. It leaves many issues that are apparently vital for faith hanging in the balance, such as the circumstances of the discovery of the empty tomb or the nature of the resurrection appearances. But further reflection shows this aspect to be its most valuable contribution. When it fails to solve the problems it raises, criticism is forced to admit its own limitations and to point to the need of something beyond itself, which for the Church at least is faith. It has the effect of divesting us of false securities which might circumvent the challenge of faith. If belief were just the response of reason to the evidence, then only reasonable men would have faith, and where would that leave the rest of us? Or again, if at the end of a scholarly discussion of the authenticity of a particular saying of Jesus, the critic has to conclude, 'I do not know whether he said it or not', then the door is open for faith to ask its own distinctive question: 'Is this consistent with what I know by experience of the character of Christ?' It is never the case that faith can tip the balance of historical uncertainty left by criticism. The facts remain historically uncertain. But where criticism is in doubt, faith can have a certainty of its own.

This is a much more frequent situation than is often admitted. When criticism has reasonable ground for believing that such and such an event happened or saying was spoken, it still leaves untouched the essential aspect of recapturing its feeling and its meaning for faith. When the critic has finished his work, he has after all to confess that his purpose at the beginning of his inquiry has failed in the end to be achieved and is in any case impossible. The best that history writing can offer is an approximation to a picture of what happened in the past in so far as it has left any trace; it can never recreate it and may therefore be totally misleading. Critical analysis and dissection require the subject matter to be kept in a state of suspended animation. But the operation is incomplete unless the patient is successfully revived! The vital experience and the totality of scripture as the source of our knowledge of God are beyond the scope of the critical method. What any single verse of the Bible or what the Bible as a whole means for faith, is a question which only faith in the community of believers can answer.

It may have appeared that to speak of scripture in the way we have done, as the sole source of Christian truth, its fountain and well, is to confine truth in a straitjacket and to neglect the possibility of discovering truth in the sciences, in philosophy or in other religious traditions. A genuinely catholic and liberal-minded Christian would be right to reject *sola scriptura* if that is what it meant. But it does not. Scripture stands alone because it witnesses to the final revelation of God in Jesus Christ. Wherever else in the world or in human experience God is truly to be found, the Christian believes that he will be like his Word revealed in scripture. This is an inclusive, not an exclusive belief. For example, when we say that salvation is through 'Christ alone' we mean by that the whole Christ, the *Christus totus*. Jesus the Messiah who died on the cross is also and at the same time the eternal Word who enlightens (anonymously, as it were) every man who comes into the

16

world, and he is the risen Lord, always present with his people in the changing situations of their history. So also *sola scriptura* must be understood as *tota scriptura*: the truth of scripture is the whole truth as well as nothing but the truth. For by its very diversity and the tensions within it, which criticism explores, it mirrors the whole of life and ceases to be a static body of literature from the past. It becomes instead the springboard of a dynamic movement, a trajectory that reaches forward into the continuing life and faith of the Church. The well becomes a fountain of truth springing up to eternal life.

FREE, BIBLICAL CATHOLICISM

I may have given the impression that the two approaches to scripture we have been considering co-exist in mutual respect and already co-operate with each other in the search for truth. Reflection on the course of the tensions and sometimes bitter confrontation between them over the last two centuries quickly dispels any illusions of this kind.[15] It is not the purpose of this book to look back to the past, but to discern signs of hope for the future; but it may be appropriate at the end of this chapter to refer briefly to the legacy left by the Oxford Movement.

The Oxford Apostles[16] had rediscovered (with an excitement understandable in a church deeply compromised in its relations with the state) the authority which is intrinsic to the Christian faith, the authority of its scriptures, creeds and councils, its spiritual life, liturgy and ministry. Not surprisingly, therefore, higher biblical criticism, with all the excesses of its nineteenth-century adolescence, was thought of negatively as a threat to faith. The heirs and successors of the Oxford Movement had to learn the painful lesson that those who have been converted from the world are often called to be re-converted, in a sense, back to the world. This was so in the case of Anglo-Catholic attitudes to political and social action. But it was also necessary in the case of attitudes to biblical criticism. Fidelity to the truth of the Incarnation, that God had

17

chosen to become involved in the ambiguous relativities of the world, led the essayists of *Lux Mundi* in 1889 towards this second conversion. Charles Gore's essay on the inspiration of scripture opened the way for Anglo-Catholicism to develop a more positive appreciation of criticism in relation to scripture and tradition. Bishop Gore later described his hope for the Anglican Church in these words:

> It was marked out to hold together the ancient Catholic tradition both in creed and order with the appeal of the Reformation to the open Bible as the final court of reference for Christians; and so to present a type of Catholicism which the world had forgotten, which should have priests but not be priest-ridden, *and should accept the Catholic tradition but keep it purged by the free use of reason and an all-pervading scripturalness.*[17]

If any proof were needed that the Oxford Movement is still as yet unfinished and incomplete, we should need only to point to the way in which his vision of a free, biblical catholicism has been eclipsed so often by extremist tendencies, both conservative and radical, in the twentieth century. Yet there is also evidence that what the Oxford Movement began may at last be achievable, in a way that its founders could hardly have anticipated. For the initiative has passed away from Oxford and largely also from Anglicanism. It is now a wider movement of the Holy Spirit within the churches to rediscover the sources of their unity in the truth, and to find in scripture, as the well and fountain of truth, the living water which Christ promised.

FURTHER READING

J. Barr, *The Bible and the Modern World*, SCM, 1973
The best modern guide to the debate on the authority of the Bible in the light of biblical criticism.
G. B. Caird, *The Language and Imagery of the Bible*, Duckworth, 1980

Illuminating applications of modern linguistic study to major issues in biblical criticism.

R. E. Brown, *The Critical Meaning of the Bible*, Chapman, 1982
This probes certain aspects of the problem from a modern Roman Catholic standpoint.

A. W. Wainwright, *Beyond Biblical Criticism*, SPCK, 1982
A Methodist approach, which finds in Jesus the criterion for biblical interpretation.

2　Images of Hope: the Old Testament

THE MEANING OF THE OLD TESTAMENT

For the first two Christian centuries, scripture was exclusively the books of the Old Testament. These writings outweigh the New Testament in sheer bulk in the ratio of four to one. Although from the perspective of faith there is a certain appeal in the plebeian roughness of Mark's style or the passionate torrent of Paul's, it has to be admitted that the Old Testament in the main is much better stuff as literature. It is also much more important material for the purposes of the historian of the ancient world, since it recounts the dealings of the nation of Israel, minor power though she may have been, with her politically overpowering neighbours, where other sources for their history are silent or fragmentary.

It is almost inexcusable, therefore, to devote only one very short chapter to the Old Testament. The length of the treatment is disproportionate to the significance which the Old Testament has both for critical scholarship and for the Christian faith. The Psalms alone are permanently etched into the imagination of church people; here truly is their book of common prayer.[1] The nobility of Isaiah, the universal appeal of the Genesis stories, the moral seriousness of Deuteronomy and the sheer humanity of Job are among the incomparable treasures of scripture. The rich variety of the Old Testament is able to embrace both the internationalism of Ruth and the patriotism of Esther, the optimism of Proverbs and the scepticism of Ecclesiastes. It thus reflects rather closely the human experience of encounter with God, which can take many widely different forms. It refuses to reduce its subject matter to the purely cultic or the inwardly spiritual, or to prescribe a mono-chrome type of the religious man.

Yet it is this very feature of Israel's scriptures that makes the question of their overall meaning so important. We cannot impose a simple scheme on such material, or trace a single golden thread through the maze which will lead us conclusively to Christ, without to some degree betraying the character of scripture. That the Church intuitively recognizes this difficulty is illustrated by the debate about the extent and order of the Old Testament canon. To put the matter briefly, the longer Greek Bible, which includes the books we know as the Apocrypha, arranges the whole collection in four divisions: Law, Histories, Writings and Prophets. It rises to a climax of expectation for the 'one to come' (Malachi 4:5): 'Behold I will send you Elijah the prophet before the great and terrible day of the Lord comes.' The shorter Hebrew Bible on the other hand has a three-part division of Law, Prophets and Writings, which implies more a decline from the beginning than a rise towards the end. Should we follow St Augustine and choose the former or follow the minority view of St Jerome and choose the latter? Our present practice of arranging the Hebrew canon in the Greek order and relegating the remaining books to a secondary status is probably the least satisfactory solution. But perhaps in doing this the Church is trying to convey that both canons have something useful to say about the meaning of the Old Testament for Christian faith.

Jesus himself may have known scripture in its Hebrew order,[2] but he was also aware of the question that underlies the Greek arrangement.[3] In the controversy on divorce, he directed the attention of his opponents to God's original decree that man should live in permanent, loving and for-giving union with his wife, which takes precedence over later legislation to accommodate human failure (Mark 10:5f). But in the parable of the murderous tenants (Mark 12:1–9) he compares the prophetic servants who were manhandled by Israel in the past with God's final appeal to respect his son. There is both a decline from the beginning and also an expectation of the end. There is both a 'proto-logical' and an eschatological unity in Jesus' reading of the Old Testament. But elsewhere there is also a recognition of the intermediate ambiguities of life between the beginning and the end.[4] Like the Dead Sea community,[5] Jesus envisaged the return of the conditions of the beginning in an imminently expected consummation, and he read the Old Testament as a book of prophecies 'for these last days'. But unlike that apocalyptic sect, he found room for the ordinary life of man in the world, for whom the Old Testament is also a school of prayer and a source of practical wisdom in the search for God and the good life. Similarly, the Christian, as he or she reads the Old Testament, should refer everything back to God as the origin of the human story and forward to Christ as the fulfilment of Israel's hope, without forcing the text into a preconceived mould or neglecting the realism and variety of its constituent parts.

When Marcion was excommunicated from the Church at Rome in AD 144, the Church committed herself to the Old Testament as Christian scripture. Marcion had objected to the Old Testament on moral grounds. According to him, its God was a severe and jealous tyrant, partisan towards the Jews and not therefore to be identified with the universal and spiritual Father of Jesus. To replace the Old Testament Marcion proposed a canon of his own, an edited version of Paul's letters with what he took to be Jewish Christian interpolations excised and an abridged copy of Luke's gospel. That Marcion exaggerated the difference between the character of God in the Old Testament and God in the Gospel, there is no doubt. That the Church was right to suspect that even more hideous perversions of the truth would result from this expedient the gnostic sects were soon to prove. But the problem for which Marcion offered such a cavalier solution did not thereby disappear.

The Church's simple assertion that 'the sacred writings were inspired of God and are able to make you wise unto salvation' (2 Timothy 3:15f) was hardly a sufficient response. Yet, without producing any particular theory of the inspiration of scripture, the Church developed a whole interpretative method to cope with the logical and moral difficulties presented by the Old Testament. The Jewish scriptures were understood in general as preparation for the Gospel, and attention was drawn in particular to explicit and implied predictions of the coming of Christ. The characters in Israel's history were seen as types and antitypes to him, and if awkward passages still remained, allegorical exegesis took over and the text, for all its literal offensiveness, was found to have the inspired word of God lying hidden somewhere beneath its surface.

These solutions coped more or less adequately with the problem until the eighteenth century. But the Enlightenment concentrated attention again on the irrational, superstitious and morally repugnant aspects of the Old Testament. In addition, the practice of historical criticism began to cast doubt upon the factual reliability of the Old Testament, and included within its scope not only the legends of Genesis, but events felt to be closer to the heart of Israelite faith, the Exodus and Sinai traditions. Opinions were revised about the dating and integrity of the books, and the assertion in the Creed 'that the Spirit has spoken through the prophets' appeared more and more to be open to question.

The reaction to these developments was first one of shock, outrage and retreat into a defensive literalism. Greater knowledge of other contemporary literature from the ancient near East, however, led to a more positive appreciation of the achievements of Old Testament writers by comparison. Moderate criticism solved more problems for faith than it raised, and cast a flood of light on passages and entire books which had previously been totally obscure and neglected. But the meaning of the whole corpus remained a problem.

It was not possible for criticism to accept as its starting point those summary evaluations of the meaning of the Old Testament that are to be found in the New Testament, implied by phrases such as 'the first Adam and the last', 'the Son of David according to the flesh', 'the Law which reigned from Moses to Christ' or 'the gospel preached beforehand to Abraham'. The proper background to schemes like these was later Jewish tradition and early Christian exegesis,[6] not the Old Testament documents in and of themselves, as criticism was beginning to understand them.

If there was to be found in the Old Testament a certain unity and an overall meaning for Christian faith, compatible with the results of critical method, the search had to begin elsewhere. Three of the principal options advocated today may be mentioned at this point. The Religion of Israel approach provides a strictly chronological presentation of the beliefs and practices of Israel in their historical and institutional contexts.[7] It deliberately avoids the question of whether there is a divine revelation in the Old Testament as beyond the scope of scientific enquiry, and concentrates attention on source-criticism of the documents and reconstruction of the forms of Israel's worship. But for all its objective rigour, this approach is able to accommodate a theory of the unity of the material, which we might call 'progress in religion'. It recognizes the importance of the emergence of ethical monotheism in Israel and the working out of the implications of that insight. That this development leads eventually to Christian faith would be seen as an accidental rather than a necessary fact; and the Old Testament as preparation for the Gospel may be qualitatively superior but is not essentially different from, say, the religious quest of the Greek philosophers which so influenced the thinking of the early Church fathers.

The Covenant Theology approach emphasizes the uniqueness of Israel's experience of God, and sees the sense of divine election as the controlling element in Old Testament revelation.[8] This allows the critic both to discover a more specifically theological unity in scripture, in the special relationship between God and Israel, and also to see this as a prefigurement of the new covenant, the special relationship between God and the Church. Such a view is more abstract than the first, less concerned to stress the connection with the cult, and less able to admit the element of radical evolution and change. Nevertheless, it discerns an apparently central and unifying motif in the Old Testament, and offers a context of understanding that is consistent with both criticism and faith.

The Salvation History approach concentrates not so much on the experience of divine election as on the remembered great acts of God by which it was established, chiefly the deliverance from bondage and the possession of the land.[9] This creed then serves as the key for the later prophetic interpretations of history, especially the experience of judgement in the exile and the hope for re-election, and thus prepares the way for the completion of Salvation History in the coming of Christ. To see the unity of the Old Testament in terms of reference to paradigmatic historical events rather than theological interpretations permits the critic to acknowledge candidly the enormous diversity of the latter in the different stages of Israel's history.

These three approaches find the centre of the Old Testament in Israel's worship of the one holy God, in the experience of covenant relationship with him, and in the saving acts of God in history respectively. The Christian reader of the Old Testament is not called upon to arbitrate in this scholarly discussion;[10] for it is clear that each approach has its own points of illumination for him. It should not in any case be expected that any one purely intellectual theory could ever capture the total phenomenon of scripture. There are certain irreducible tensions in scripture as in life, between the memory of the past and the immediacy of the present, from which a synthesis is possible only at the level of experience.

The unity to be found in the Old Testament, we might say therefore, has more than one central focus. There is perhaps an analogy here in what Christians have wanted to say about the unity of God: that he is transcendent over creation and history, yet immanent within human experience and 'incarnate' within human history, and that these are not three different and competing activities of God but three ways of speaking about one and the same activity.

IN THE BEGINNING

The community of faith reads scripture as a book about God; it refers everything back to God's initiative, to find its origin and meaning there. The biblical critic may want to express the matter in a slightly different way, and say that the Old Testament is a collection of writings which illustrate the range of beliefs about God in Israel at different stages of her history. But he would not disagree that the final purpose of this literature is to proclaim the initiative of God. Whatever other purposes are also observable (political propaganda, moral education, spiritual counsel or even popular entertainment) belief in God is always the first cause of the writing down and of the preservation of scripture. There may be scholarly dispute, as we have seen above, about the proximate origin of the belief that there is one God. We may, for instance, emphasize the breakthrough achieved by the eighth-century prophets and purified further by their later followers, or we may want to tie the writing prophets back into the community tradition which they inherited. We may try to trace the belief in the oneness of God to a unified concept of nature celebrated in the cult, or to the unique effectiveness of Israel's divine sovereign, revealed in historical acts of salvation. But the ultimate origin of the belief that God is one is the self-revelation of God: this is what the Church insists upon as the real meaning of the Old Testament. The chronological order in which these human perceptions occurred does not affect the truth that in the beginning is God.

The scholar interested in the history of religions will ask whether this is a natural or a historical 'beginning', so that he can classify the Old Testament on one or other side of that basic divide. But it is not only practically impossible to answer the question in the case of Israel, it is also theoretically impossible. The very name which God reveals as his own implies this. In Exodus 3:14 the significance of the name 'Yahweh' is given in God's reply to Moses: 'I AM WHO I AM'.[11] Israel's God is self-defining and uniquely self-revealing. If the name originally meant 'the one who brings into being' we still cannot tell whether it is the created order, or the elect people or the victories of Israel's armies which he brings into being. God is the beginning in a higher sense, which makes it illegitimate to ask what in particular he begins. Within the Old Testament, the emphasis may fall in one place on history and in another on creation. The records of the Judges and Kings of Israel are left without integration alongside the natural theology of the early wisdom books. The priestly redaction of the Pentateuch (late sixth century) produces a kind of synthesis by supplying a cosmological preface to its corpus of revealed law. Creation may sometimes be seen as historical combat, or deliverance in history as an act of creation.[12] But whatever constitutes the focus of immediate attention in any of these writings or in any section of them, the reality of God transcends it. The parallelism of creation and historical redemption, and God as the beginning of both, is, I should say, the most distinctive feature of Israel's mature faith.

The ordinary reader of the Bible, whose confidence in the reliability of the historical assertions of the Old Testament has been shaken by rumours of what criticism is saying, may feel more at home with the biblical emphasis on God as creator. He or she may point to the first paragraph of the Creed to support that preference, and be willing to suspend belief in whether, as a matter of fact, God performed signs and wonders in the wilderness, or said anything to Moses on Sinai clearly enough for it to be written down. But on reflection it becomes clear that creation in and by itself is no less ambiguous than history as evidence for the existence of God. Neither can by-pass the need for faith. There is no easy resolution of the ambiguity of nature. We could say that creation is both very good, because God has made it and also full of pain, because man has marred it. But it would be equally true to say that the world is *full* of pain only for the man who suffers innocently in it, and that it cannot be *very* good by existing for man's convenience but only by being itself. When creation alone is taken as the meaning of the Old Testament, the focus quickly becomes blurred.

Christian readers of the Old Testament, therefore, are bound to pay attention to history, not merely because it provides the framework and the largest part of the contents of it, but more importantly because this history is their own history; it is the story of the Old Testament Church. For a gentile to become a Christian, as Paul says, is to be grafted as a wild branch on to the olive tree of Israel's election, and to share its sap. 'And if you are tempted to feel superior, remember that it is not you that support the root, but the root that supports you' (Romans 11:17f). And the reader makes this story his own by entering into it. This does not involve the uncritical acceptance of the historicity of certain events in the past, but an act of faith which transposes them into the present. Biblical criticism has shown that Old Testament writers themselves saw the Exodus event in this way. When Deuteronomy says that God 'led you these forty years in the wilderness' and in all that time did not allow 'your clothes to wear out or your feet to swell', (8:2 and 4) he is addressing a congregation centuries after the time when that bedraggled and foot-sore few managed to survive the great trek through the desert. In his book *Life Together*[13] Dietrich Bonhoeffer makes the same point thus:

> Forgetting and losing ourselves, we too pass through the Red Sea, through the desert, across the Jordan into the promised land. With Israel we fall into doubt and unbelief and through punishment and repentance experience again God's help and faithfulness. All this is not mere reverie, but holy, godly reality. We are torn out of our own existence and set down in the midst of the holy history of God on earth.

And he continues:

> It is not that God is the spectator and sharer of our
> present life, howsoever important that is: but rather
> that we are the reverent listeners and participants
> in God's action in sacred story. Only in so far as we
> are *there*, is God with us today also.

The function of the history in sacred scripture is, then,
to 'tear us out of our own existence', and it can accomplish
this whether or not it is historically factual in all its detail.
Exodus is an act of God's grace and initiative; it has its
beginning in God. When that truth is forgotten, even the
Exodus can become relative and ambiguous.

> Are you not like the Ethiopians to me,
> O People of Israel, says the Lord.
> Did I not bring up Israel from the land of Egypt,
> *and* the Philistines from Caphtor,
> and the Syrians from Kir. (Amos 9:7)

If the Exodus points back to God as its beginning, it is
also seen as pointing forward to the future, when God may
surpass it. The prophet Jeremiah saw the return from exile
in this way. 'The days are coming,' he wrote, 'when men
shall no longer say "As the Lord lives who brought up the
people of Israel out of the land of Egypt," but "As the
Lord lives who brought up and led the descendants of the
House of Israel out of the North Country and out of all
the countries where he had driven them".' (Jeremiah 23:7f.)
That the new Exodus of Jeremiah turned out to be historically as ambiguous[14] as the critics allege the old one was,
does not alter its meaning for faith.

All this is not to say that faith remains impervious to
the results of historical enquiry. Certain accounts of the
Exodus,[15] if critically proven, would make it unreasonable
and inappropriate to see that event as a paradigm of God's
initiative in the way Israel saw it, just as some theories
about the circumstances of Jesus' crucifixion and the

29

origin of the belief that he had risen from the dead are incompatible with faith.[16] But a critically sober account of the facts in either instance cannot ever compel faith, or it would not be faith.

The Old Testament teaches us that God is the beginning of creation and of history, and that the reality of God is not only revealed in them but exists beyond them. Thus a space is left for critical enquiry, the same space which is needed for faith.

DECLARING THE END FROM THE BEGINNING

The Church reads the Old Testament as a book about Christ; it refers everything forward to what God accomplished in him. The unity and overall meaning of scripture is then found by reference to its end, the fulfilment of its promise in the coming of the Messiah. From the day of Pentecost until the modern period, a running battle on this question has been raging between Jewish and Christian biblical commentators. The issue between them is neatly summarized in the eunuch's question after he had read the fourth servant song in Isaiah 53:

> As a sheep led to the slaughter
> Or a lamb before her shearer is dumb,
> So he opens not his mouth.
> In his humiliation justice was denied him.
> Who can describe his generation?
> For his life is taken up from the earth!

He asks: 'About whom, pray, does the prophet say this, about himself or about some other?' (Acts 8:34) All the wealth of Ethiopia could not compare with the hidden treasure that Philip bestowed upon him then. 'Beginning with this scripture, he told him the good news of Jesus' and baptized him into the people of God. Biblical criticism, however, suspects that the Ethiopian may have been short changed, and has more often than not come down on the side of Jewish commentators on the issue of messianic prophecy.

The expectation of a Messiah, an anointed king in the line of David, cannot be said to be a leading motif in the Old Testament. It is largely a post-exilic phenomenon, and achieves its clearest expression only in post-biblical Judaism. Some messianic texts like the Apocalypse of Ezra[17] did gain access to the larger Christian canon of scripture, but since that work was composed around AD 100, it can hardly be said to point forward to the coming of Christ. Prophecy after the event, indeed! Other works like the Psalms of Solomon,[18] which are thoroughly messianic, remained outside both the Hebrew and the Greek canons. Messianism is not an invariable feature even in inter-testamental writings; many know nothing of it. The paucity of material is reflected in the New Testament itself, where texts which had no previous connection whatever with the hope for a future Son of David are given a messianic reference for the first time.

The Israelite monarchy is the biblical basis for Messianism and it is a curious institution. Since 'God is the King of all the earth' (Psalm 47:7) there might seem to be little room in Israel for any other. When the people clamoured for the reflected glory of kingship, the prophet warned them of the awful consequences of their request before acceding to it (1 Samuel 8). Hosea expressed the ambiguity of the institution in these words: 'I have given you kings in my anger, and taken them away in my wrath.' (Hosea 13:11) Popular enthusiasm on the occasion of coronations and royal weddings evoked expressions of unvarying divine favour on the dynasty, which were formally inconsistent with a proper sense of covenantal obligation and in the event historically refuted. Material of this kind such as Psalm 2 and Psalm 110 did not historically mean what the New Testament writers later took it to mean by connecting them with Christ's baptism or his resurrection. But, then, it did not really 'mean' what the critics tell us it was actually saying at the time. For to speak of a minor oriental despot as 'begotten of God' and 'seated at God's right hand' is palpable exaggeration.

The disappointing performance of David's successors

produced a credibility gap between the theory and the practice of monarchy so large that the exalted language of kingship began to be cast in the future tense. Isaiah prophesied the birth of a child who would represent a sign of God's presence with his people in the person of a new heir to the throne: 'Behold a young girl shall conceive and bear a son, and shall call his name Emmanuel' (Isaiah 7:14).[19] But again, the hope ran ahead of the achievement even of Hezekiah, and the prophecy remained available for any later application that might be found for it. The future restoration of the Davidic dynasty appears in the writings of the exilic prophets as part of a general restoration of all Israelite institutions; and in Zechariah 9:9 it is stripped of its military and royal aspects:

> Rejoice greatly, O Daughter of Zion!
> Shout aloud, O Daughter of Jerusalem!
> Lo, your king comes to you;
> triumphant and victorious is he,
> humble and riding on an ass.

Israelite monarchy thus begins in compromise and finishes in paradox.

The proclamation of the Kingdom of God in the teaching of Jesus is just as important as fulfilment of Old Testament messianic hope as the Church's proclamation of the kingship of the risen Christ. For the former reverses the compromise while the latter resolves the paradox. If God alone is king, then one of two consequences might be thought to follow. Either his earthly representative must be one who outstrips all others in his obedience to God's rule, and 'does not lift up his head above his brethren' (Deuteronomy 17:20). Or else he must be given the same honour as the one he represents, sharing his unconditional authority, and 'anointed with the oil of gladness above his fellows' (Psalm 45:6f.). The Old Testament, as we have seen, was undecided about which of these was the more appropriate deduction. It could not envisage the possibility, realized in the person of Jesus, that both might be.

It is not merely this monarchical strand that the Church is thinking of when it speaks of the witness of the Old Testament to Christ. It is also the much more widespread element of inconclusiveness, which we may indeed claim to be a regular feature of the Old Testament and one which points to the coming of Christ as its conclusion and fulfilment.

The history of Israel itself peters out quite remarkably after the exile and is left without a conclusion. No one dared to offer an explanation of what was happening to God's people. There is an exception that confirms the rule in the period of the Maccabees. But even there apocalyptic interpretation like Daniel's, which lays some claim to divine authority, shelters behind the inspiration of a figure from the past and hedges its bets with the ambiguity of multivalent symbolism. And the straightforward history of the period is nervous and self-distrustful, wine and water stuff, on its own admission (2 Maccabees 15:39) not strong enough to upset the stomach or inflame the passions.

In the sphere of worship, Israel had recognized the inevitable tension between the outward practice of the cult and the call to inward devotion. But the issue became more and more polarized, with the post-exilic elaboration of the priestly regulations on the one hand, and the hope for a future purification of the Temple and its priests on the other.[20] There was a similar tension between the election of Israel to be the people of God's own possession and the sense of a mission to the world, expressed in the prophecy, 'My House shall be called a house of prayer for all nations' (Isaiah 56:7) which hardens later into an increasingly exclusivist nationalism.[21] The inconclusiveness of the Old Testament is evident also in the theme of suffering. All the elements of the problem are present in the literature, but 'dismantled', so to speak, waiting to be assembled into a coherent instance: the vicarious suffering of the Servant of Yahweh, the martyr creed of Daniel's saints, figured like a Son of Man anticipating vindication, and Job's vision of God refined by his pain.[22]

That the Old Testament is a body of literature without

a conclusion is not a perception of Christians alone; Jews and Moslems share it, on the evidence of the Talmud and the Koran. And biblical criticism endorses the truth of the observation by its marked preference for the period of Israel up to the exile and its comparative inability to make sense of the tail end of the Old Testament.

Of course, criticism is right always to warn us against reading the text of scripture anachronistically, as though the fulfilment were already present. But that is no part of the Christian case. The biblical expectation of one to come, the Messiah in the widest sense of the word, is just a pile of hopes and images until the coming of Christ. And the cross of Christ negates them in their obvious, literal sense. 'Jesus of Nazareth, a prophet mighty in deed and word before God and his people . . . our chief priests and rulers delivered up to be cruficied. But we had hoped that he was the one to redeem Israel' (Luke 24:19f.). But the coming of Christ also fulfils expectations, in an unexpected way perhaps, and in a way which entails the need for faith certainly; and in him the hopes and images of the Old Testament are purified and reborn.

THE VALUE OF THE PENULTIMATE

We have seen that the unity and meaning of Old Testament scripture arise from referring everything to the beginning in God and the end in Christ. According to the book of Revelation, God and his Christ together are 'the Alpha and the Omega, the beginning and the end', and as such they give to the thirsty 'water without price from the fountain of the water of life' (Revelation 21:6, cf. 22:13 and 7:17). But the Old Testament has another dimension important for faith, its emphasis on the reality of the intermediate. In many places it is preoccupied not with the alpha and the omega but with the beta pluses and minuses of life, the decent second-class concerns of ordinary people. The Christian reader in his eagerness to push on to earth-shattering truths may fail to detect in these sections those hairline fractures in the fabric of experience which are also capable of allowing the water of life to filter through. The Old Testament, diligently used, is the perfect cure for such impatience.

Let us briefly consider just three examples out of many. The Law of Moses contains, along with those stirring moral insights of universal significance, apparently trivial regulations which seem to have no value as a source of spiritual refreshment. But their very detail represents a truth, that God's law covers not just the theory but also the practical working out of it in far from clear instances. In Deuteronomy 22:12 the instruction is given, without explanation, that 'tassels should be worn on the four corners of the cloak', a rule which Jesus himself faithfully observed (Mark 6:56). The same legislation in Numbers specifies that blue cords should be attached to the tassels, and also adds a partial explanation, that this practice should be a reminder of the requirement of obedience (Numbers 15:37–41). There is no mention of the origin of the convention, which is hardly surprising if the critics are right that the custom is a piece of primitive magic to ward off evil spirits. But the wearing of tassels on the cloak becomes a sign of submission to God's law.

Convention is a prime example of what we refer to as the penultimate, and the law of tassels illustrates that it also has its place in the divine economy. Strangely enough, it is when the Law speaks of higher things, and adds explanations and motivations for obedience, that its status as law becomes most problematical. 'You will wear tassels' is more appropriate to the legal form than 'You will love your neighbour as yourself.' It is precisely when the Law thunders from Sinai rather than quietly arranging matters here below, that man feels most helpless to respond to it. But while the word is merely on the edges of your garments, it can be obeyed. The value of the penultimate remains and there is liberation to be had in simply doing what you are told.

The Hebrew text of Job is in almost as pitiful a state as its chief character, covered with sores. One such is that famous text in 19:25f:

For I know that my redeemer lives,
And at last he will stand upon the earth.
And after my skin has been thus destroyed
then from my flesh I shall see God.[23]

The RSV margin notes: 'the meaning of this verse is uncertain', but the Christian reader is far from uncertain. For him the clouds have suddenly parted to reveal Christ and the resurrection as the answer to all Job's problems, only to close again immediately afterwards and become overcast for the rest of the book. But, instead of rushing to our conclusion, there is value in remaining for a while in the ambiguity of the present, and listening to those critics who suggest that the verse is really a piece of cruel irony rather than a sudden, unaccountable infusion of faith. Job knows that there is someone around who could stand up for his righteousness, against those who try to find the secret sin in him that has led to such a punishment, and he will come forward; only it will be too late then. What good is it to the innocent sufferer to know that his reputation will be rehabilitated after death? If anything, it makes the pain worse. It is in the flesh that Job wants his vision of God to be restored. When flesh turns to dust there will be no chance of that. This is not an unchristian reading of our uncertain text. For Jesus no more than Job could look death in the face and smile in the hope of vindication. The reality of death, which above all confines men in the penultimate, cannot be evaded by an easy victory. Resurrection is always an act of God's grace, and not a human certainty that can be cashed out in advance to cope with the adversities of life.

My last example is that strange bedfellow for the rest of the Old Testament, the Song of Songs. Jewish as well as Christian exegesis has traditionally taken it as an allegory, whether of Yahweh and Israel or of Christ and the Church, and thus sidestepped the difficulty of explaining how an erotic love poem managed to gain admission into the canon of scripture. But the enjoyment of human love, another primary instance of the value of the penultimate, is the plain sense of this book, and is, as Bonhoeffer once remarked, 'probably the best christological exposition of it, too' (*Letters and Papers from Prison*).[24] He expands on this cryptic remark in another letter.[25]

> God requires that we should love him eternally with our whole hearts, yet not so as to compromise or diminish our earthly affections, but as a kind of *cantus firmus* to which the other melodies of life provide the counterpoint. Earthly affection is one of these contrapuntal themes, a theme which enjoys an autonomy of its own. Even the Bible can find room for the Song of Songs, and one could hardly have a more passionate and sensual love than is there portrayed. It is a good thing that that book is included in the Bible as a protest against those who believe that Christianity stands for restraint of passion (is there any example of such restraint anywhere in the Old Testament?).

The intermediate ambiguity of scripture which we have been considering in the examples of convention, death and love, does not detract from its centres of unity which we looked at before, God its beginning and Christ its final end. But over these underlying unities and in harmony with them, the Old Testament builds up a counterpoint of human concern with the penultimate in all its variety.

FURTHER READING

F. Stolz, *Interpreting the Old Testament*, SCM, 1975
A simple but not simplistic introduction.
W. Schmidt, *The Faith of the Old Testament*, Basil Blackwell, 1983
A recent and admirable survey of the Old Testament.
J. Sawyer, *From Moses to Patmos*, SPCK, 1977
This explores the meaning of the different parts of the Old Testament in relation to the whole.

3 The Word Incarnate: Jesus and the Gospels

THE FOUR GOSPELS

There is only one Gospel, and yet there are four New Testament gospels. In this apparent contradiction lies one of the reasons why faith and criticism are both necessary in the Christian use of scripture. We cannot simply identify the Gospel with the written gospels, because the Gospel is one. Yet the four gospels are the chief witness to the one Gospel of Jesus Christ.

The last statement is not really as self-evident as it appears, and it is useful to consider its implications. At certain periods in the Church's history the theological teaching of the Apostle Paul has threatened to replace the gospels as the centre of the Christian Bible. The stories and sayings of the earthly Jesus, contained especially in the first three gospels, have been reduced to almost the same level as the Old Testament and treated as preparation for the post-Easter message of the Gospel.

The very word 'Gospel' might at first appear to support the precedence of apostolic preaching over the written gospels. Before the New Testament period, the Greek term 'evangelion' had a rather limited, secular meaning, to do with the public announcement of political events, like the birth of an heir to the throne or success in a military campaign. The verb 'to herald good news' is rare in the Greek translation of the Old Testament, but it is used in the later sections of Isaiah (61:2) in reference to the work of the prophet anointed by God's Spirit to preach the good news of release to the Babylonian exiles. According to Luke 4:18f., Jesus applied this prophecy to his own ministry, and to the situation of his hearers, when he was asked to read in the synagogue at Nazareth. At first then the 'Gospel' meant the oral proclamation of deliverance, and the Church understood Jesus' death and resurrection in particular as the events which accomplished it, and which extended the message of salvation to all mankind. On this view, the Gospel cannot be disconnected stories about Jesus' earthly life, even less a biographical collection of them. It has to be a direct appeal to faith.

However, the four gospels are indeed the chief witness to the Gospel. The liturgical practice of the Church has maintained their centrality for faith in Christ. This is vividly symbolized by the way they are read in Church, especially in the Eucharist. Often the reading is accompanied by ceremonies which derive in part from the practice of the ancient synagogue, and imply that the four gospels have acquired that authority for Christians which Jews accord to the five books of Moses. The people stand to hear the Word of God; the gospel book is carried in procession, consecrated with lights and incense, intoned by the deacon and reverenced with a kiss. The gospels are a sacramental sign of the presence of Christ in the community and are therefore to be treated with similar respect to that rendered to the consecrated bread and wine in the second part of the liturgy. It is not at all surprising that gospel criticism appears to many as a sacrilege. The words and deeds of God Incarnate are not to be prodded and probed by the unsanctified hands of the critics. The Gospel comes not to be criticized but to criticize and to call us to repentance and faith.

But if we recognize the truth of both our propositions, that there is one Gospel and also that there are four gospels, that there is unity and plurality at the same time, we shall not be able to exempt the one Gospel from historical criticism by dissociating it from the four; nor to exempt the four gospels from criticism by simply identifying them with the one.

In the course of the second century AD, the word

'gospel' began to be applied to texts. But the texts were held to witness to a truth that went beyond them; they did not supply a complete definition of it. This is clear from the way they are referred to, not as the Gospel *of* Matthew, Mark, etc., but the Gospel *according to* them. There were, in fact, many so-called gospels circulating at this period, the surviving fragments of which may be found in the New Testament Apocrypha.[1] Some of them belonged to the category of romantic fiction, while others were more like philosophical treatises. The four gospels which came to be included in the New Testament stand head and shoulders above these aprocryphal works, and established themselves by liturgical and doctrinal use in different parts of the Church. But instead of allowing one of them finally to predominate, the Church endorsed all four.

There was an element of historical accident in the number which is scarcely disguised by the famous comment of St Irenaeus that the four gospels correspond to the four winds and corners of the earth.[2] The four living creatures around God's throne envisaged by Ezekiel (1:10) and elaborated in the book of Revelation (4:6—7) were increasingly taken by Church Fathers as justification of the plurality of the gospels. They had some difficulty, however, in decoding the symbols and deciding whether Mark was the eagle and John the lion or vice versa, and why Luke was the calf and Matthew the creature with a human face! Whatever fanciful explanations were offered for the plurality of the gospels, the fundamental reason for adopting all four was the perception that the truth of the Gospel, although one, has many facets and the evangelists each in their own way have light to shed upon it.

The observed differences between the four gospels nevertheless remained a real problem. They were not gross discrepancies in theological interpretation, such as may be found occasionally in the Old Testament,[3] but minor variations in fact which required considerable ingenuity on the part of Christian commentators to explain. One solution, proposed by the apologist Tatian, who flourished around AD 160, and adopted in his native Syria for several centuries after him, was to harmonize all four into one continuous narrative, the *Diatessaron*.[4] The more common alternative was to rely on exegesis to account for the disagreements. It was possible to argue for multiple performances by Jesus of the same action like the cleansing of the Temple, or his use of the same or slightly variant sayings on different occasions during his ministry. Or else, allegorical exegesis could be used to explain apparent contradictions of fact as examples of inspired theological comment.[5] The case of the fourth gospel over against the other three was more difficult, but not insuperable. For John provided the inner spiritual truth to complement the outer 'bodily' information given by the others. Thus, the Church was reassured of the truth of her gospels. The record was true history and the way it was presented was a single and true interpretation. The evangelists had been given a special charisma to preserve them from error. They were next to God's throne, flying with the wings of the Spirit, and full of eyes outside and inside to perceive the truth in all its aspects (Revelation 4:8).

The plurality of the gospels is still the major problem faced by critical scholarship today. It lies at the root of all the methods which we currently use in studying the gospels: source criticism, form criticism and redaction criticism.[6]

Source criticism is the study of the literary interrelationship of the gospels. The discovery that Mark's gospel was the first to be written and was used as a source by Matthew and Luke has the initial effect of unifying the synoptic tradition. The variations in wording or order from Mark can be credited to editing by the later evangelists. But source criticism worsens the problem in two other respects. To explain the common material in Matthew and Luke which does not result from their use of Mark, it is often felt necessary to postulate the existence of a sayings document 'Q'.[7] This hypothetical reconstruction has a format and emphasis which are strikingly different from Mark's. The latter concentrates on the deeds of Jesus leading up to the Passion, the former on his words pointing forward to the future coming of the judge and king of the final age, the Son of Man. The second respect in which this method exacerbates the problem of plurality is that it isolates the fourth gospel from the others. Concentration on sources makes John appear eccentric and out of line.

Form criticism is the attempt to go behind the written texts of the gospels and recover the forms or units of oral tradition from which they are thought to be made up.[8] It relates the structure of these to the setting in the life of the earliest communities which handed them on and adapted them to their needs at the time: preaching, worship, catechism, debate and so on. This method also seems to unify the gospels by demonstrating that they are constructed from the same building blocks. Even parts of the fourth gospel can be seen to display this characteristic. But equally this method disintegrates the tradition and raises the problem of a plurality within each gospel. The miracle stories, for example, are set in almost irreconcilable opposition to the controversies on points of Law. And the more sceptical form critics like Rudolf Bultmann[9] go so far as to suggest that the miracles represent a picture of Jesus as a Hellenistic wonder worker, and the controversy stories represent him as a Jewish Rabbi; neither of them is true to that eschatological prophet from Nazareth who preached the Kingdom of God in parables.

On the form critical view the synoptic evangelists were merely collectors and editors of widely diverse traditions. They did very little themselves by way of producing a coherent picture of Jesus. In recent years this has been increasingly challenged by the redaction critics.[10] They restore theological unity to the synoptics and thus bring them closer in intention if not in style to the fourth gospel. But the problem of the plurality of the gospels increases on this view, because each evangelist, they claim, has made a distinctive composition out of the common stock. Often, one evangelist's position is characterized by reaction and opposition to his predecessors. Matthew disputes Mark's doctrine of the hidden Messiahship of Jesus, while Luke rewrites the whole story to conform to a different, longer-term conception of world history, toning down the primitive expectation of an imminent end. It is not our purpose here to enter into a detailed discussion of the methods of gospel criticism, but to illustrate a general problem in the use of the Bible, the need to perceive its unity without neglecting or underestimating its pluralism.

What is the unity of the gospels? We could answer that they find their unity in reference to Jesus, and in their value as evidence for his life and history. But the quest for the historical Jesus has produced a huge variety of possible reconstructions.[11] Although some are more plausible than others, it is inconceivable that the Church would ever replace her four gospels with an authorized, critical biography of Jesus. By definition, such a biography would not be a gospel. For it would have to distinguish what actually happened or was said from what those who witnessed it understood to be its meaning, whether at the time or retrospectively in the light of its eventual outcome.

We might try to claim, by contrast, that the unity of the gospels consists in the faith held in common by the communities from which they arose. We could claim that they believed Jesus to be Messiah and Son of God (Romans 1:3—4); that he had been crucified and raised from the dead (1 Corinthians 15:3—4); and would come again soon as judge and saviour (1 Thessalonians 1:10). But if we take these quasi credal summaries culled from the epistles as our starting point, and make the earliest form of preaching or 'kerygma',[12] as it is called, our criterion of unity, the bulk of the contents of the gospels will have to be deemed irrelevant and indeed a dangerous and misleading distraction from the central issue.

Alternatively, we could follow the recent trend and admit quite frankly that neither the Jesus of history nor the common faith of all early Christians can be rediscovered with any certainty. It would then be the chief task of criticism to give an account of the gospels in their present form — of which we do at least have direct knowledge. What results from this trend is four different interpretations of Christ, each having a coherence of its own, perhaps, but

43

having no coherence as a set. The gospels may tell us what their authors individually believed, but not what we ought to believe, nor why these particular interpretations should be given the kind of absolute precedence which the Church awards to them.

Consequently, the unity of the gospels cannot be found exclusively in their reference to the historical Jesus, nor in their context within the faith of the Church, nor in the theologies of the gospel writers. All three dimensions must be included, if faith and criticism are both to be adequately served. The same point can be put in another way. The unity of the gospels comprises the Word of God preached by Jesus, the Word of God which is the message about Jesus, and the Word of God which Jesus himself is. It is normal to refer to the last of these ideas alone, in theological shorthand, by the term 'Incarnation', and to distinguish it sharply from the first two, the preaching of Jesus and the Church's proclamation of his death and resurrection. On this view, the 'Incarnation' must be judged a peripheral concern of the gospels, limited to a few passages of John which display a developed understanding of the nature of Christ's own person. It does not include his teaching or his work. But even the fourth gospel speaks not of an incarnation of God, but of the Incarnation of the Word. And when equal emphasis is placed on both parts of the formula, it can indeed be seen as a summary of the central concern of all the gospels. The teaching of Jesus, his life, death and resurrection, no less than the Christian understanding of his person are instances of the Word Incarnate, the true focus of unity within the plurality of the gospels.

THE WORD OF GOD

Before I continue to elaborate this way of understanding the unity within diversity of the gospels, it may be useful to trace some of the biblical background to the notion of the Word of God. The power of words in religion is well illustrated by two types of genuinely 'performative utterance', the blessing and the curse. Once spoken, they are thought to have automatic and material effect. They fly through the air towards their targets, and can be countered only by diversionary action, not by cancellation. This conception is present in Israelite religion also, and even in the record of Jesus' ministry.[13] But its crude magical element has been purified by the recognition that it is not the incantation of certain words as such which is powerful, but Yahweh, who channels their force according to his will.

The Word of God spoken to the prophets was understood not as a static revelation of his eternal character, but as a dynamic expression of his will. The Lord put forth his hand and touched the mouth of Jeremiah and said:

> Behold, I have put my words in your mouth.
> See, I have set you this day over nations and over
>   kingdoms,
> to pluck up and break down,
> to destroy and to overthrow,
> to build and to plant. (Jeremiah 1:9f.)

The power of the Word of God realizes itself in actual events. A dramatic illustration of this is found in the so-called 'prophetic signs'. In the book of Ezekiel, for instance, the prophet is told to shave his hair, and to burn, scatter or chop up parts of it and hide just a few locks in the skirts of his robe. The fate of the people is sealed in a symbolic act: 'Thus says the Lord God: This is Jerusalem' (Ezekiel 5:5). The Word of God, unlike the noises uttered by men, effects what it signifies. It is always cast in the imperative mood. Not only history, as the arena of God's judgement and salvation, but the whole created order results from his Word. In the beginning God said 'Let there be light, and there was light' (Genesis 1:3). The Word in creation, sent out to melt the snow and ice and cause the rivers to flow, is connected in Psalm 147:16f. with the Word of God revealed to Israel in the Law. The Word is not truly God's until it ceases to be verbal and becomes an actual state of affairs. So, the Word of God could be said to have a tendency to 'incarnate' itself in the concreteness of the created order and in the occurrences of history.

I must be careful here to avoid special pleading, and to explain what I mean by a tendency towards incarnation. In one sense incarnation language is peculiarly Christian, and at odds with the Old Testament contrast between human flesh and the Word of God: 'All flesh is but grass . . . the grass withers, and the flower fades, but the Word of our God will stand for ever' (Isaiah 40:6,8). And there is an element of deliberate provocation and polemic in the assertion of John's prologue that 'the Word became flesh and tabernacled among us' (John 1:14).[14] The Jewish tradition understood God's glory dwelling as in a tent among his people to be the Law. John accordingly divests the Law of its transcendent, saving aspects, its grace and truth (John: 1:17), and reinvests Jesus with them.

In another sense there is in the Old Testament idea of the Word of God a genuine prefiguration of the Christian doctrine of the Incarnation. Despite the primitive origin of the idea and its conditioning by specific features of Israelite tradition, it contains a permanent insight into the nature of God's dealings with the world. There are two sides to it. In the case of men, their words are the outward expressions of their thought; in the unique case of God, what is the expression of his thought, if not the world and its history, what is and what happens? And yet, God as creator must transcend his own creation, and leave it to be itself. The created order is not a figment of God's imagination, and it demonstrates its capacity for independence by frequently disregarding his will. Israel came down firmly on the side of realism, and against any kind of pantheism or idealism. So it is possible to claim that in creation and history God simultaneously expresses and hides himself. As an expression of his power and his Word, he allows other things to exist where before only he existed; he stands back from what he himself has made and gives it breathing space.

The paradox of God's simultaneous transcendence over and immanence within his creation is graphically presented

46

in the figure of personified Wisdom. Proverbs says of Wisdom:

> The Lord created me at the beginning of his work,
> the first of his acts of old . . .
> I was beside him, like a master workman;
> and I was daily his delight, rejoicing before him always,
> rejoicing in his inhabited world and delighting in the
> sons of men. (Proverbs 8:22, 30)

Wisdom is the cheerful labourer who admires the designer and loves the work. In later Jewish tradition, Wisdom is associated even more intimately with the being of God, no longer a creature as in Proverbs, but 'an emanation of the divine glory' (Wisdom of Solomon 7:25f.). But she is also associated even more closely with the daily affairs of men, not just their creation. Identified with the Law (Sirach 24:23), she dwells among God's people, attracts them by the beauty of virtue, and communes in particular with the wise and righteous among them (Wisdom of Solomon 9:10). In her function as agent of creation and revelation, she resembles the Word of God. It is only in the role of judgement that a female personification is considered slightly less appropriate than the image of the Word, 'a stern warrior who leaps from God's throne in heaven . . . filling all things with death and touching heaven while standing on the earth.' (Wisdom of Solomon 18:16) With the coming of Christ as a man, it was natural to translate the Wisdom language generally into the masculine gender and to speak of him as the Word.

There can hardly be any doubt that it is this tradition which is the direct precursor of the exalted language of pre-existence applied to Christ in the New Testament. Speculations about the influence of the so-called gnostic redeemer myth are anachronistic.[15] The gnostic doctrines of the second century and later are derived, sometimes in a deliberately de-christianized form, from the New Testament itself. They are also unnecessary. With such a rich vein of scriptural material to work on, Paul or John would hardly have needed to pick up hints from the sort of syn-cretistic nonsense allegedly propagated by their opponents.

What is so surprising, in view of all this, is not the presence of such 'incarnational' motifs in the New Testament, but their comparative absence and the extreme reticence with which they are employed. The gospel writers must have been aware that over-concentration on the Wisdom background would have prevented them from conveying the different 'levels', if we may speak in this way, at which the Word was incarnate in Jesus. It is quite clear, for instance, that Matthew knows and accepts the characterization of Christ as the Wisdom of God. He allows an echo of the Old Testament figure to come through in Jesus' invitation:

> Come to me all who labour and are heavy laden,
> and I will give you rest.
> Take my yoke upon you and learn from me;
> For I am gentle and lowly in heart,
> and you will find rest for your souls.
> For my yoke is easy and my burden is light.
>
> (Matthew 11:28—30)[16]

He speaks of Jesus' ubiquitous, spiritual presence where two or three are gathered for prayer in his name (Matthew 18:20). And he happily correlates the Son with the Father and the Spirit in the baptismal formula at Matthew 28:19. But there is no mention of Christ's pre-mundane activity in creation or redemption, and if it were not for a few texts like these we might have concluded that Matthew's assessment of the status of Jesus is 'lower', as they say, than John's, and even perhaps, in its emphasis on the traditional category of Messiahship, 'lower' than Mark's. The writers of the synoptic gospels, therefore, must have deliberately refrained from expressing fully their own convictions about the person of Jesus in order to allow his message and his life to speak for themselves.

I argued above that the image of the Word of God serves both to identify the world and the history of his people as

48

the work of God's hand, and also to secure his distance and sovereignty over it. In his Word God is simultaneously expressing and hiding himself, communicating with and standing back from his own creation. Thus, the image contains an element of unfulfilled hope. For it leaves open the possibility that God might in one instance perfectly express and perfectly hide himself.

The pious Jew at the time of Jesus recited three times a day the Shema': 'Hear, O Israel, the Lord thy God, the Lord is one, and you shall love the Lord your God with all your heart, and with all your soul, and with all your might' (Deuteronomy 6:4—5). The practice is continued in its Catholic Christian form in the threefold daily Angelus. When the church bell is rung, the faithful recall the Incarnation of the Word of God 'made known by the message of an angel'. What the Church believes about Jesus is that at a particular moment the course of history was reversed. By God's grace the Virgin stood aside in order to allow God to be within his own creation in a final and complete way, when she said: 'Behold the handmaid of the Lord. Be it unto me according to thy word.'

In the following three sections I intend to explore the different ways in which it is possible to speak of the Word incarnate as the unifying centre of the gospels. The message of Jesus is the Word which 'incarnates' or insinuates itself into the human situation in the form of parable. The story of Jesus' life, death and resurrection is Word incarnated and made present for us as liturgy. The person of Jesus is the Word of God made flesh for our salvation according to the dogma of the Incarnation.

PARABLE

I have followed the normal usage earlier of referring to the 'teaching' or 'message' of Jesus which criticism has some-times attempted to reconstitute for us from the text of the gospels. But this usage is misleading. There is no one, simple doctrine that can be extracted from the words of Jesus. The amateur rabbi and humane prophet of Nazareth was an unsystematic and occasional teacher whose view of God and the world was indeed profound and compelling but was hidden in a complex of poetic stories and analogies.

It is this fact alone that explains the remarkably slight influence which the teaching of Jesus has had on the formulation of Christian theology, starting with Paul. When the sayings of Jesus are detached from their larger context in the story of his life, and an attempt is made to organize them into a theology, the result has always been bizarre, as the Church was to realize early on with the gnostic heresies. If 'Q' ever existed, it was a collection of *obiter dicta*, and it is not without significance that it has failed to survive. Its form as a collection would have been a betrayal of the character of its contents. The influence of Jesus in Christian doctrine may be small, but his influence on Christian spirituality can never be overstated; the gospels translate into prayer even when they cannot be fitted into theology.

Professional theologians, unlike ordinary believers, have not been able to reconcile themselves to this fact.[17] Faced with the difficulty of distilling doctrine out of Jesus' words, they have tried instead to read doctrine into them, chiefly by allegorizing the parables. The haunting beauty and exciting freshness of Jesus's storytelling, which attracted such large audiences to him and marked his use of parable off from the conventional cleverness of the scribes, was almost smothered by the allegorical method. The parables of Jesus have an internal life and impact of their own, which is lost when their individual features are decoded piecemeal. St Augustine's famous exegesis of the parable of the Good Samaritan managed to squeeze the whole creed and half the catechism into the text, but failed to capture the feeling and reality of the story.[18]

It is sometimes claimed that the allegorical interpretation attached by Mark to the parable of the Sower (Mark 4:13–20) has the same effect, but this is only partly true. Certainly, Mark is pursuing his own theological interest by extending the category of 'riddle' (appropriate to sayings like Mark 7:15) to cover the parables as a whole. He wishes to explain why it was that the Jews rejected Jesus as their Messiah, and he does this here by supposing that Jesus taught in riddles in order deliberately to keep the truth from them, and so to allow the gentiles to enter the vacuum left by their unbelief. The allegory of the Sower is very likely to be secondary, a product of preaching in the community, but its aim is not to read later doctrine into the story, but to point out how this and all the other parables are to be heard, that is receptively and with a pure heart. I take that to be a faithful interpretation of Jesus' original intention, which criticism is only just rediscovering and faith has always known.

We ought to notice that the Sower is not identified, and what he sows is simply called the Word (verse 14). No definition of the content of the Word is given, for the community refuses to detach the call to repentance or the announcement of the nearness of God's kingdom from the person and work of Jesus himself. And the Word is 'implanted' in those who receive him (cf. John 1:12f.), which is what we mean when we speak of 'incarnation' in our present context.

The parables of Jesus as living story involve the listener in active participation in the construction of their meaning. As the critics have demonstrated, the parable of the Sower is a natural tale; it stays within the bounds of ordinary experience. It is confusing and unnecessary to add moralizing definitions of the birds of the air, the thin soil and the thistles, as the devil, persecution and the riches of this world respectively. But the critics have been just as keen as the old allegorizers to find doctrine in it. They usually see the great harvest as a symbol of the Kingdom of God, to which the loss and wastage of sowing is the prelude and literary foil. Having thus dispensed with the husk of the parable, they can proceed to discuss the doctrinal kernel, and ask whether in the teaching of Jesus the Kingdom is the imminently expected end of the world which Jesus merely heralds, or the present possibility of grace in fellowship with him which Jesus offers, or a little of both.[19] But the impossibility of finding definitive answers to such questions has forced critics more recently to retrace their steps and attend again to the parable itself.

Why does the story expend so much energy on describing the hazards of sowing, if the point is really the harvest? The farmer may be following the ordinary Palestinian custom of sowing *before* ploughing, but other oddities remain. Why does he not bring his children out to scare away the crows? A good farmer knows his land like the back of his hand, as they always tell us, and would know to avoid any hidden shelves of rock. And why does he not burn the thistles and dig out their roots before he begins? What was missing in the earlier interpretations which is at last receiving more attention is the reaction of the hearer as an integral part of the parable: the reaction of disapproval at the Sower's crass incompetence, which turns to outrage at the undeserved windfall of his final harvest. The Kingdom of God is indeed implicated in this parable. It actually arrives as the Word takes root in the heart of the listener and accuses him of begrudging the generosity of God.

In the same way, the Good Samaritan (Luke 10:30–7) as parable has the effect of forcing itself into the life setting of the hearer.[20] Critics who believe that Jesus' parables all refer to a future Kingdom tend to down-grade material like this to the category of 'example story' and even to question its authenticity.[21] Those who support the idea of a present kingdom are on much stronger ground here, but the lesson they draw from it is usually weak and moralizing. In neither case is the structure of the story itself sufficiently taken into account. The narrative begins in a way that allows the listener to run ahead of it. Hearing of a priest and a levite who failed to help, he naturally expects the hero to be a Jewish layman. When he turns out to be a Samaritan, a half-breed and a heretic, he is momentarily disoriented and is compelled to identify thereafter with the Jew in the ditch, as the recipient of grace. Salt is rubbed into the wound by the provocatively unreal picture of a totally available Samaritan who has unlimited leisure and resources to indulge his charitableness. The Word is incarnated in the sense that it is impossible to crystallize out the 'message' of the parable verbally. The Word becomes flesh in the response of the listener, who feels himself being drawn into the reality of the story.

These brief examples must suffice. But before we leave the subject of parable, we need to say a little more about the Kingdom of God. An incompatibility has sometimes been alleged between the teaching of Jesus on this subject and the incarnational doctrine of the Church.[22] The Kingdom of God, whether understood in an inward and moral sense or in a future, apocalyptic sense, is incompatible with any idea of mediation. The transcendent theism taught by Jesus is then diametrically opposed to the later Christian proclamation of Christ as God's vice-regent and mediator of salvation.

This is an extreme and simplistic distinction which the majority of critics have refused to follow. For a start, it makes any continuity between Jesus and the community that claimed him as its own historically inconceivable. More particularly, it disregards hard textual evidence which contradicts it. Only those who adopt a position of almost total scepticism with regard to the historicity of the synoptics have denied that there must be some connection between the proclamation of the Kingdom of God and the identity of the one who proclaimed it. Some such saying as the following must be original: 'Whoever is ashamed of me and of my words in this adulterous and sinful generation, the Son of Man will be ashamed of him when he comes in the glory of his Father with the holy angels.' (Mark 8:38)[23]

We may want to deny that Jesus identified himself as God's future vice-regent and deputy-judge; we may very plausibly argue that 'the coming of the Son of Man' is a figurative way of speaking about God's own Judgement in the future. But what we must admit is that Jesus believed the future judgement was being pre-determined by the reaction of men to his words here and now. The Word as agent of God's judgement is thus operative in advance of the last assize. To pursue this line of argument further would take us too far from the issue in hand. But it may be useful to state what I believe to be the significance of Jesus' language about the Kingdom of God, and how its coming is related to the parables.

The evidence of the gospels, critically assessed, does not support the view that one simple, coherent notion is present in every example of the phrase. There is a whole variety of connotations which correspond quite closely with the various ways the language of God as King is used in other Jewish literature at this period. What is unusual is the application of apocalyptic imagery to what we might call the existential experience of encounter with God in the present.[24] In other words, the traditional and rather complacent notion of God's eternal sovereignty has been shaken and revolutionized by talk of the sudden arrival of his Kingdom. That this is parable or metaphorical language is clear from the high level of verbal inconsistency to be found in it. 'The Day' or 'the Kingdom' or 'the Son of Man' comes preceded by warning signs, wars and rumours of wars (Mark 13:7), or it comes without observable signs, in a time of false peace and security (Luke 17:20ff.). It may come as a thief in the night (Matthew 24:43) or as a bridegroom in the night (Matthew 25:6), as an image of terror and loss, or of joy and consummation. That Jesus was in agreement with the vast majority of his contemporaries, Jewish and pagan alike, in believing that the world had only a limited future, we do not for one moment doubt. But it is very doubtful whether the literal end of the world is the referent of Jesus' highly varied and verbally inconsistent language about the coming of the Kingdom.

As we have already seen, parable is a non-negotiable feature of Jesus' teaching. We cannot elbow it out of the way and lay our hands on the pure doctrinal content. We cannot translate it into plain speech; on the contrary, it translates us, the audience, into its own reality. Thus, parable creates its own end, its Eschaton, of judgement or of grace, in the life setting of the listener who participates in it. The Kingdom comes in a 'speech-event' and thus cannot be detached from the Word and the one who pronounces it. In the parable itself this world disappears and a new world is brought into being, and the real meaning of that saying becomes apparent: 'Heaven and earth may pass away, but my words will never pass away' (Mark 13:31).

LITURGY

It is no small part of the genius of biblical faith, in both the Old and New Testaments, to present its truth in the form of story. Whatever may be true about God in himself, man is essentially a being with a history. He lives in time, within a process of change and in community with other beings similarly conditioned. He cannot become aware of God and remain at the same time entirely true to himself, unless God's self-revelation is mediated to him dynamically and narratively.

Story is a type of incarnate word. In a story the words do not remain verbal, they become flesh in the movement of the narrative and in the imagination of the hearer. This is a feature of story in general. It is particularly true of the gospel story, because it has the quality of finality, the story that puts all others into perspective and into the shade. The Christian reader listens to the drama of Jesus' life, death and resurrection against the background of the images of hope in the Old Testament. This background, whether assumed or made explicit by the narrator, gives the tale its finality, and creates recognition and fulfilment. But, as we have seen, fulfilment in this case is not limited narrowly to one strand of Old Testament hope. The nationalist expectation of a Davidic Messiah is exploded before being reassembled in a new form. The predominance of the themes of healing, moral goodness, betrayal and suffering have the effect of universalizing the story and making it the tale of Everyman.

An interesting example of this tendency is the evangelists' use of the Son of Man as a self-designation of Jesus. By and large they do not try to insert into their accounts the post-Easter titles, Christ, Lord and Son of God. They allow a confusing variety of estimates of Jesus' person to remain in their texts, including what must be considered inadequate descriptions of him: rabbi, teacher and prophet. But they all equally follow what must have been a literary convention in early Christian storytelling of making Jesus refer to himself as the Son of Man. We can show by comparison of the gospels that the phrase has sometimes been added by an evangelist.[25] But he is not reflecting, as we might expect, the later christology of the Church, since the Son of Man is never found (in early Christian literature) as a title of dignity or a confession of faith.

The phrase has its ultimate origin in the idiom of Jesus himself, but criticism has uncovered several different meanings in it. Sometimes it is used as the standard poetic way of referring to man (e.g., Mark 2:28). Sometimes it may be a cautious periphrasis for the speaker himself in contexts where politeness or squeamishness forbids a first-person pronoun (e.g., Mark 8:31).[26] Sometimes it is used in quotation marks as an allusion to Daniel 7:13f. and is probably taken symbolically as the victory of God's elect people and the defeat of their enemies (e.g., Mark 13:24). What the evangelists appear to have done is to run these different elements into a single description of the significance of Christ as the one who fulfils the destiny of man. This is not a piece of theoretical christology, overlaid on the text. It always points the reader back to the narrative to find there what Jesus means by calling himself the Son of Man.

We have been considering the gospels as story, making their impact on the reader precisely through their narrative form. They convey salvation not as a set of propositions which the believer is called upon to accept with just the top of his head, but as a living and moving drama in which he becomes an active participant, not a passive spectator. This understanding of the gospels has been reinforced by the findings of critical scholarship. The order in which the evangelists place the brief units of tradition that are available to them is dictated not so much by consideration of strict chronology as by their feeling for dramatic effect. As an example we might consider this passage:

56

O Jerusalem, Jerusalem, killing the prophets, and stoning those who are sent to you. How often would I have gathered your children together as a hen gathers her brood under her wings, and you would not! Behold, your house is forsaken and desolate. For I tell you, you will not see me [again] until you say, 'Blessed be he who comes in the name of the Lord.'

Matthew places this (23:37—9) in the Temple itself, with Jesus surrounded by a hostile audience of scribes and Pharisees, still smarting from his attack on their hypocrisy. He is just about to leave for the Mount of Olives where, overlooking the city, he will describe in detail its desolation. His triumphal entry has already occurred (21:9) and the final statement thus becomes a promise of his glorious second coming. St Luke, by contrast, places the passage much earlier, at the point of Jesus' unceremonious departure from Galilee, threatened with death by Herod and yet aware of even worse things that have to be faced in Judaea. From Luke 9:53 onwards Jesus has Jerusalem fixed as a picture in his mind, and he looks forward to his arrival there, when he will be greeted with blessings from the crowd (19:38) before he suffers the fate of all the prophets. At that later point, Luke recalls the earlier incident: 'As he drew near and saw the city he wept over it, saying "Would that even today you knew the things that make for peace! But now they are hid from your eyes" ' (Luke 19:41). Both versions make good dramatic sense; neither finds any reason in the implications of the words 'How *often* would I have gathered, etc.' to question Mark's design of a single, climactic visit to Jerusalem, or to follow John's arrangement which has frequent, lightning visits to Jerusalem when Jesus attended the major feasts.

Many other examples might have been chosen to illustrate the way material is ordered dramatically by the evangelists. The chronological and slight verbal discrepancies between the gospels cease to be a problem for faith on this view. We accept the legitimacy, which for the gospel writers is a necessity born of factual ignorance, of four

57

different versions of the same basic plot. We read and appreciate each in its own terms, and we read the four together as a set, in order to gain that insight into the story they are telling which may enable us to compose our own. To use the jargon of the modern communications industry, redundancy is the solution to interference.[27] Saying something more than once ensures that no part of the message essential to its meaning as a whole will be lost.

We have been using the term 'story' to indicate how history becomes effective in the present. Perhaps a better term for this function of the gospel narratives is liturgy. Liturgy is a dramatic re-presentation of the story of salvation within the community of faith. Individual passages of the gospels are, of course, read in the liturgy, but in addition the whole sweep of the story is presented liturgically in the festivals of the Church's year. The attention of the worshipper is concentrated on one particular moment in the life of Jesus, his birth, baptism or transfiguration, in relation to the climax of it, his death and resurrection, which always form the centre of the celebration. In Holy Week the events of Jesus' Passion are followed in sequence on consecutive days and the character of the liturgy as sacred drama becomes unmistakable.

This use of the story of Jesus in the liturgy has more than religious psychology to defend it. It has a solid critical and historical basis. In the early Eucharist, the Lord's death was remembered and 'proclaimed till he comes' (1 Corinthians 11:26). The critics tell us that it was very likely this remembering and proclaiming in the context of worship which gave rise to the formulation of the Passion story, first orally then in written form. The gospels then resulted from extending the Passion backwards in time and supplying it with an introduction, explaining who Jesus was and why he was suffering. The proclamation of the Lord's death was the interpretative frame around the symbolic actions of the Eucharist: the breaking of bread, the pouring and blessing of the cup, and the common meal. The story gave the sense of the actions, and the actions 'incarnated' the words.

This may help to explain why there is less emphasis than we might have expected on the resurrection in the gospels, especially Matthew and Mark, and much sharper divergence between them on the details of the Easter events than we find earlier in the Passion story.[28] When the gospels are read as story, they need a proper ending. The resurrection of Jesus is the grand finale and climax, and time is needed to assimilate it and begin the process of reviewing everything that has gone before in its light. But when the Passion is used as liturgical story, it naturally stops short of the resurrection. For its function is to proclaim the Lord's death, a historical event about to be re-enacted symbolically in the breaking of bread. In this context, it would be dramatically inappropriate to anticipate the outcome. The death of Jesus is mediated to the community by an act of remembering, but the resurrection of Jesus needs no such mediation. The risen Lord is really and immediately present in the communion of his body. Thus, Mark seems to have ended his work where the liturgical tradition finished (16:8) or he may have rounded it off with a brief concluding sentence which later scribes found inadequate and replaced.[29] Matthew's ending is the minimum required to close the account, but is at odds with Luke at all the significant points, the number, location, character and content of the appearances. John's gospel agrees more closely with Luke's but has an appendix (chapter 21) which harmonizes with Matthew's and expands on it.

The Christian reader may at first be dismayed by all this, and feel that the witness of the gospels is weak where it most needs to be strong. But the liturgical character of the gospels points in the opposite direction; the apparent lack of unanimity in their endings is due not to the weakness, but precisely to the strength of early Christian faith in the resurrection of Jesus. The reality of the experience of the risen Christ in worship made fixed records of his appearances unnecessary.

So far we have looked at parable and liturgy as examples of the 'incarnation' of the Word. It is now time to remove the quotation marks and consider the dogma of the Incarnation.

59

DOGMA

It is vital to be clear what we mean by dogma. For the word is popularly misunderstood as a prejudice, above reason and beyond criticism. But the original Greek word means simply an 'opinion', with the overtone of authoritative opinion. In early Christian usage it comes to signify a decision of the Church in council, a decree which 'seemed good to the Holy Spirit and to us' (Acts 15:28 and 16:4). In arriving at its conclusion, a council listens to the evidence of scripture and the arguments of theologians, and searches for the common mind of the Church: a search which is not complete until the decision has later undergone a process of 'reception' by the whole People of God. With these qualifications, dogma is held to be a truth revealed by the Holy Spirit. The dogma of the Incarnation was defined at the Council of Chalcedon in AD 451 and the main elements of the definition are contained in the Nicene Creed. What difference should this make to the Christian who reads the gospels today?

First, it does not at all imply that the evangelists must be thought to have already perceived the truth in the same form in which the Church later defined it. If that were the case, it would not have been necessary to define it as a dogma. From the fact that the heretics were themselves using the text of the gospels to support their views, the Church was well aware of the ambiguity of the evidence of scripture. What it proposed was that there was one person of Christ, fully God and fully man. The alternatives it rejected were that there were two Christs, the human one inhabited by the divine, or that there was one semi-divine Christ disguised as a man. The unity and reality of Jesus forbade the first, and the unity and reality of God forbade the second. The witness of scripture to the Incarnation was confirmed by the experience of the Church in prayer and in the sacraments. In short, what the Church's dogma of the Incarnation does is to insist on the mystery of the person of Christ, and outlaw superficially more logical views which dissolve the mystery.

The dogmatic reading of the gospels, therefore, is not opposed to a critical reading of them. It recognizes the ambiguity and open-endedness of the evangelists' perception of Christ, and indeed safeguards it against those who offer more clear-cut solutions. It allows St Mark to ask his question after the stilling of the storm: 'Who then is this, that even the wind and sea obey him?' (Mark 4:41), and justifies his failure to provide an answer to it.

The dogmatic reading is a reading of the gospels continuous with the Church's tradition. And it has to show that what was later understood to be the meaning of the gospels is not inconsistent with them but a proper development from them. Several criteria are used to test whether the development is proper. They include the Church's experience of Christ in prayer and sacraments as well as scriptural exegesis and theological argument.

Recent study of the synoptic gospels by the method of redaction criticism has warned us not to make over-hasty deductions about the evangelists' own views simply from the contents of their work. We have to distinguish between the tradition which they rather conservatively hand on and the often discreet but highly significant redactional contribution. We might consider, for example, the implications for Luke's christology that he has Elizabeth say to Mary before Christ is even born: 'Why is this granted me, that the mother of my Lord should come to me?' There are behind the synoptics certain unspoken axioms, prior conceptions about the person of Christ, which the writer and his readers share and against which the rest of the text is to be interpreted.

The fourth gospel is much more explicit in its view of Christ and is often claimed as self-evident support for the Church's dogma. But it was also claimed as self-evident support for various heretical views — a fact which caused some delay in its acceptance as canonical by the Church. The fourth gospel certainly supplies some of the vocabulary for later discussion when it says 'The Word was made flesh' (1:14), but the original intention of that language was not theological definition. For John's prologue, we must remember, is a hymn. It is poetry not philosophy, and its reference to the Word become flesh is paradoxical and polemical. The poetry contains a touch of satire against those who exalt Wisdom and the Law over Christ, the true saviour of the world.

The fourth gospel may explore the mystery of Christ, it does not explain it. When Jesus is referred to as the Word, the door (10:9) or the way (14:6) he is thought of as the means of the revelation of God, a window through which men may see the invisible Father. It is as though Jesus, fleshly and opaque as a man, is at the same time transparent of God. Just as Jesus the Word incarnate reveals God, so the Spirit in the post-Easter community, the Paraclete (14:25), reveals Jesus. The Spirit is given to remind the disciples of what Jesus had said and done on earth, and to lead them into fuller truth about it. He speaks in the community through inspired preachers and apologists, especially the one whose sermons have been included in the gospel itself as discourses of Jesus.[30] Thus the Spirit in the community leads believers back to Christ, and Jesus as the Word leads them back to the Father.

John's theology has no speculative intention. That was the mistake the heretics made. Its purpose is pastoral. It proposes a solution to the problems which faced his church, the problems of how to distinguish true spirits from false within the community, and how to distinguish true interpretation of Jesus from false in the debate with the synagogue.[31] John's view of Christ is therefore not identical in form or intention with the dogma of the Incarnation defined at Chalcedon, but the Church is surely not wrong to claim that it is consistent with it and developing towards it.

The Christian who reads the gospels dogmatically, in the light of the Church's teaching that there is one Christ fully God and fully man, is not acting out of prejudice except in the sense that he is accepting the prejudgement and accumulated insight of the community to which he belongs. This judgement is still open to be tested by critical study and also by reference to the consistency of the dogma with present experience in prayer and worship. And the way it is to be applied to the text is not predetermined. The dogma predicts a conclusion; it does not prescribe a method. On issues such as whether Jesus mis-remembered the name of the High Priest in the time of David (Mark 2:26) or was unable to perform miracles in Nazareth (Mark 6:5) the gospels must be allowed to speak. Limited knowledge and limited power are so much a part of what it means to be fully human that it would be inconsistent with the Incarnation to excise their evidence. Similarly, criticism must have its full say on the correctness of Jesus' beliefs concerning the future of the world, or whether he walked on water or changed it into wine. The dogma does not permit all miracles and all divine insight to be denied to Jesus *a priori*, but it leaves particular instances open to enquiry. For the Incarnation embraces both the cross and the resurrection, both the expression of God's power in total human weakness and also the divine victory over death and the grave.

We have claimed that the doctrine of the Incarnation is a focus of unity with which the gospels are read in the community of faith, and have tried to indicate how this may be compatible with acceptance of the findings of criticism. The second and equally important function of dogma in the Christian reading of the gospels is a negative one. It puts an end to speculation. Dogma forbids the arrogantly inquisitive to probe into the mystery of Christ, a search which would lead them away from worship and faith. The inner consciousness of Jesus and the nature of the Son's pre-existence are fruitless questions from the point of view of faith and are totally beyond the range of sober criticism. The dogma of the Incarnation provides the useful function of warning that this is a 'No through road'.

For this reason, if for no other, it is regrettable that the word 'myth' has been introduced recently into the discussion of our subject.[32] Myth in the sense, say, of the gnostic myths, speculations about the pre-earthly career and inner life of the Redeemer and of those he redeems, is precisely what dogma is designed to combat. In the New

Testament we are mercifully spared those intoxicating flights of fancy about the pre-existent Christ and the psychology of the incarnate Christ, which have always left theologians in the end peering over the brink into an abyss. The early Christians, like the Chalcedonian definition, stop at the paradox and turn to worship. The synoptic gospels give us the outward and objective evidences of the incarnate life of Christ, and the fourth gospel when it speaks of his inner being does so in a way that makes it a vehicle for revelation, not a subject for speculation. In Jesus' prayer to the Father in John 17, there is no introspection. The attention of the reader is drawn away from the motives and feelings of Jesus in himself towards the glory of the Father with whom he is perfectly one, and the work of salvation he has been given to do on the earth.

The dogmatic reading of the gospels is the opposite of a speculative reading, whether mythological or humanistic. The question it asks is not what was it like to be Christ, which is spiritually unhelpful and critically unanswerable, but what on this evidence is God like, and what is true manhood like?

THE CHURCH

The community of faith interprets the gospels with reference to its own context, conditioned by its own corporate life and its sacramental forms of worship. But is this the proper context for understanding the gospels? Critical study has shown that the evangelists and the tradition they were using were themselves conditioned by their context in the Church; but it has questioned whether it is correct to confine Jesus himself in this way. It is argued that his fore-shortened view of the future of the world, and his belief in its imminent end, made it unnecessary to set up institutions to survive his death and continue his work.[33] The Church and the sacraments were not envisaged by Jesus, and we fail to understand him properly if we interpret him ecclesiastically.

This challenge to the way in which Christians read

scripture is a powerful one and deserves more serious treatment than we are able to give here. Certainly the breadth of worldly interests in the gospels, as in the Old Testament, forbids a narrow ecclesiasticism, but the fundamental issue is whether an incarnational understanding of salvation, corporate and sacramental, does justice to the intention of Jesus. I shall make just a few, brief observations on this.

In the first place, eschatology, the belief that this is the final epoch in the history of the world, is a way of expressing the importance of time and the reality of earthly existence. The horizontal distinction between the present and the future is far less damaging to the institutions of catholic Christianity than the vertical distinction between the visible and the invisible, matter and the spirit. The disappointment of future hope in the second century, the apparent failure of the End to arrive, did not create the institutional and sacramental Church. It was in being long before. It gave rise to the spiritualizing sectarianism of the gnostics.

Second, it is probably correct to say the Jesus did not *found* the Church. But this is not because he preached a Gospel to the isolated individual. His understanding of salvation was a thoroughly corporate one, because the Church already existed, in Israel, the people of God. What Jesus looked forward to in the future was the renewal of Israel, and he symbolized in advance this hope by appointing the twelve as new patriarchs to rule with him in the age to come (Matthew 19:28). He promised Peter that he would be the foundation of a new people (Matthew 16:16–18).[34] The Church is not wrong to apply Jesus' teaching to itself as the community of salvation. The Church goes wrong only when it applies this to itself as it is, rather than to what by God's grace it is destined to become.

Third, the same observation applies to the sacraments. Jesus did not institute Baptism, he received it from John, in the expectation that the water rite would be fulfilled by a baptism in the spirit which was still to come in the future. His table fellowship with his disciples on the night before Passover was a traditional and inherited sacrament which he anticipated would be fulfilled in the Kingdom of God. His way of salvation was thoroughly sacramental, but the rites of the Church are only part of its realization. The sacraments are the outward signs not only of inward grace, but even more of future glory.

The corporate and sacramental understanding of salvation, on the basis of which the Church interprets the gospels, is a faithful reflection of the teaching of Jesus and a consequence, as we shall see, of the doctrine of the Incarnation. In this chapter I have attempted to show that the gospels, for all their plurality, have their unity in the Word Incarnate. Jesus' parables, the story of his life and his own person all witness to one Gospel, the coming into flesh of the Word of God.

FURTHER READING

J. A. T. Robinson, *Can we Trust the New Testament?* Mowbray, 1977
 A very readable introduction to the problems raised by criticism.
C. F. D. Moule, *The Birth of the New Testament*, A. & C. Black, 2nd ed., 1966
 The best study of the factors contributing to the writing of the New Testament documents.
E. Franklin, *How the Critics can Help*, SCM, 1982
 A thoughtful discussion of the effects of criticism on the pastoral and liturgical use of the gospels.

4 Believing in the Body of Christ: Paul and the New Testament Canon

THE EPISTLES OF PAUL

The letters of Paul are the most extraordinary component of the Bible. They are the oldest surviving Christian literature and are first-hand testimony of an identifiable and important figure from the earliest days of the Church. They are therefore an invaluable source for the historian of the origins of Christianity, but are they scripture?

Paul clearly did not intend his letters to be scripture, but that does not settle the issue. None of the New Testament writers intended to compose scripture; for scripture was the Old Testament. The only exception to this is perhaps the book of Revelation, which claims for itself a kind of scriptural integrity (see Revelation 22:18–19); but, ironically, this was the last work to gain entry into the New Testament canon and the one which encountered the strongest resistance. The writings of the New Testament became Christian scripture because they arose out of the life of the community and were endorsed as authoritative through liturgical and doctrinal use by the community. But the letters of Paul are the product of one individual, who is frequently at odds with those he is addressing. And they probably had less impact on their original recipients than they had later on people who knew nothing of the particular problems with which they deal.

The letters are the work of an apostle, or at least of one whose claim to be an apostle, despite his former career as a persecutor of the faith and his ignorance of the earthly Jesus, was upheld by the Church. But do the remarks of an apostle on any subject whatever become *ipso facto* scripture? Paul's letter to Philemon, for example, is an appeal to a friend to be generous in the treatment of a runaway slave (verse 10) and a request for overnight accommodation (verse 22). What makes this holy scripture?

It is not even the case that Paul wrote his letters from deliberate choice. He was forced by circumstances, bad weather and travelling difficulties, illness and imprisonment to communicate with his congregations by means which he considered second-best to direct personal contact. From the earlier and longer period of his career (AD 35–51) no letters are known. Paul picked up his pen in every case to respond to particular situations or requests for guidance from his churches. We have no way of knowing now what those situations were except through the hazardous procedure of reading between the lines of the letters themselves. Depending on how we reconstruct the other half of the conversations, the significance of Paul's words changes dramatically. For example, he begins his discussion of marriage and celibacy at 1 Corinthians 7:1 with the words: 'It is well for a man not to touch a woman.' Is this the point which Paul chiefly wants to make in this chapter? Or is he here quoting an opinion expressed in the Corinthians' letter to him? Or had the Corinthians been quoting Paul's own words back at him and misinterpreting them out of context? How many sets of inverted commas should we put round them in our punctuated translations?

The train of thought is hard to follow, not only because of our ignorance of the situation Paul faces, but also because of Paul's own habit of mind. Paul can break into song, or invective or biographical anecdote as the mood takes him. His thought in places is so disordered that some critics with tidier minds than Paul suspect his letters have been cut up and put back the wrong way. There is such variety in the opinions he expresses, bordering on self-contradiction, that some have doubted whether one person could have written them all, and others have tried to account for his changes of mind and mood by positing a rapid evolution of his thought in the last ten years of his life.

As genuine letters, Paul's writings are ephemeral and highly personal compositions. They draw a vivid picture of his own personality, and they usually pass the test of the ancient Greek stylist who remarked: 'The beauty of a letter lies in the affection and courtesy it expresses.'[1] But the same writer went on to warn against writing letters on heavy subjects more suited to a treatise. Keep it light, was his advice. Proverbs and popular wisdom are acceptable, but 'a writer who expounds general reflections and urges a way of life on you is not chatting with a friend in a letter but preaching *ex cathedra*.' In disregard of literary propriety, Paul frequently becomes weighty and strong. He expounds the meaning of faith in Christ with a maturity and depth that has perhaps never been surpassed. His letters may be deficient as literature but they contain sound teaching. Is this what makes them Christian scripture?

In a later section of this chapter we shall see how the New Testament canon itself provides an answer to our question, but first we shall consider the evidence of the epistles themselves. We shall assume that the critics are right to cast doubt on the Pauline authorship of the epistle to the Hebrews, which claims no such authority for itself. We also agree that the three pastoral letters to Timothy and Titus are expansions by a later author of fragments that derive from Paul. The case of Ephesians is more difficult, and criticism is very divided, so it is safest to delay consideration of it until later. We are thus left with nine letters written to various small and scattered communities in Asia Minor, Greece and Rome in the intervals between his visits to them.

PAUL'S JUSTIFICATION

The question is, what makes the letters of Paul scripture? The answer normally given, especially in the churches of the reformed tradition, is that Paul teaches the true faith, in his doctrine of justification. For this is said to be the heart and soul of the Gospel. A man is liberated from guilt, and the power of sin and the prospect of eternal punishment, by the free gift of God in the atoning death of Jesus, and to this he responds by faith alone.

Some startling conclusions follow, if we accept this as the correct answer. Not only should Paul be admitted into scripture, he should be given the first and highest place in the canon. For he teaches clearly a doctrine which is at best merely implicit and at worst blurred and obscured in the four gospels. Second, it is not all of Paul's letters equally that should be given precedence, but only those which teach justification by faith. Of these, Galatians and Philippians contain allusive summaries. It is only in the first half of Romans that we find a full exposition. (It would be better not to include chapters 9 to 11, for there Paul lapses into a Jewish concern with God's promises to his elect people, which he ought to have realized were out of date.) Thus, scripture has been whittled down to Romans 1—8, Paul's *summa theologica*. A third conclusion from this premise would be a revised view of the nature of tradition. The language of justification by faith is notoriously absent from the working vocabulary of the Greek Fathers; they and their later successors were more concerned with the doctrines of the Trinity and of the person of Christ. The true Gospel of justification seems to have gone underground shortly after Paul, to resurface momentarily in the works of St Augustine, and to be brought back to the light of day only at the Reformation. Of course, such drastic conclusions about the content and structure of scripture, and its relation to tradition, have rarely been made explicit. But they are the logical consequence of supposing that Paul's place in scripture is owed to the enduring truth of his doctrine.

However, this kind of truth should not be expected from the Bible. If it is a well and fountain of truth that lies beyond it, it is not a repository of true statements that can be appropriated at their face value. There are, no doubt, many true doctrines to be found in the letters of Paul, but that is not why they are counted as scripture. There are many false doctrines and several errors of fact in different books of the Bible, but that does not make them any less scripture.

The critic, no less than the ordinary Christian who has never really understood the technicalities of justification, has good cause to be alarmed by this reductionist and simplistic treatment of scripture. The historical circumstances in which Paul was forced to express the truth of Christ in terms of justification by faith cannot be discarded as irrelevant to its meaning for us today. The letter form in which the doctrine is presented in all its original particularity ought to guard against such an error. In his dealings with the churches of Galatia, Paul realized that the most determined opposition to the Gospel was — as he himself had reason to know well — that which emanated from the envious and fanatically Pharisaic mission among Jews of the dispersion. This combined active persecution of those Jewish Christians who were trying to retain membership of the synagogue alongside their new faith, with profound theoretical objections to the preaching of a crucified Messiah. The threat of persecution was used to blackmail Jewish Christians into advocating compromise over the circumcision of their gentile breathren.

Paul was not against compromise as such, as long as it furthered the spread of the Gospel (1 Corinthians 9:20—2), but this particular demand, if made an absolute precondition for membership of the Church, would have smothered his mission in the cradle, and turned Christianity like Pharisaism into a sect for the devout few, and not a way of salvation for all mankind. Persecution was the price that the Jewish followers of the Crucified had to pay in order to bring life to the world. In the debate the Pharisaic missionary held up Abraham as a model for the would-be convert to Judaism to imitate, for he was justified by his obedience to God's Law and showed the strength of his commitment by accepting the pain of adult circumcision. Paul replied by claiming Abraham as a convert, before his time, to the true faith of Christ (Galatians 3:16). The patriarch was first justified by faith (Genesis 15:6); his circumcision was a secondary detail. The Pharisee retorts that such a doctrine cheapens God's grace, makes no demands on human response and is a religion without tears. Paul's answer is that it is not cheap grace if it led Jesus to the cross, and it is costly enough to any Jewish Christian who pays the price of persecution for the sake of the freedom of the Gospel.

Paul had time to reflect on the extremism of his language about freedom in Galatians, and the way his words were being twisted by false friends (Romans 3:8); but he stood by what he had said and refused to be ashamed (Romans 1:16). In the first part of Romans he turns to confront his chief opponent in this debate, the persecuting Pharisee, the ghost of his former self. And he sets out to destroy all his old arguments and take every thought captive to Christ. The Romans themselves must have been just as puzzled when they read this amazing letter as every ordinary reader and every scholarly exegete has been ever since. The theology cannot be detached from the controversy and the personality of the controversialist. Paul tears himself apart in front of his readers, and shows them the agony and the glory of his apostleship. The individualism of Romans 1—8 is Paul's own; it is not a blueprint for ours. The corporate understanding of salvation in Romans 9—11 is not an appendix, it is the climax. It is what Paul wants gentiles in Rome and everywhere else to hear in what he was saying.

The historical circumstances of Paul's letters, therefore, make it illegitimate to extract phrases from them as the basis of a theological system. Furthermore, Paul was himself an unsystematic thinker and was content to be ambiguous, as scripture generally is, at points where theology prefers clarity. To take just one example, some modern theologies, influenced especially by existentialism, have tried to find meaning and relevance in Paul by starting from what he says about man, his anthropology.[2] But if we look at the two passages where Paul draws a parallel between Adam and Christ, the first man and the last, we quickly discover that Pauline anthropology is not coherent enough to form the basis of a theology. In 1 Corinthians 15 Paul compares the creation of Adam, the man made out of dust, with the resurrection of Christ, the man from heaven. The perishable and mortal nature of the first man is contrasted with the imperishable nature of the risen body of Christ. The man of dust was subject to disintegration in death because of the friable stuff of which he was made, not, interestingly, because of his fall into sin. In this passage Paul speaks of man's mortality, in agreement with the majority of Jewish theologians at the time, as his *natural* condition, and not as a punishment, for one very obvious reason. Death was not enough of a punishment! It was merely a brief reprieve before man faced the real consequences of his sins at the resurrection to judgement.

In Romans 5, however, Paul adopts for the sake of argument a different view from the one presupposed earlier. This is a minority opinion of a particularly gloomy and deterministic kind which argued that all men are subject to death as punishment for Adam's primal sin. The context of this use of the parallel between Christ and Adam is a discussion on the Law, and Paul is making a point *ad hominem* against those who claim that the Law alone can save us from an otherwise inevitable fate for which we are only partly responsible. He asks in effect: If we adopt this view, does the Law make any difference? Is fallen man any less subject to death because of the giving of the Law? Not at all. For, as everyone knows, men after Moses live even shorter lives than the patriarchs who preceded him. Nothing can stop the encroachment of mortality, then, except the hope of resurrection with Christ, as Paul goes on to explain in his next chapter. Thus, Paul does not have a fixed view of the relation of sin and death, which is a crucial point for any anthropology. He does not have a fixed view of man to which his doctrine of salvation in Christ is the answer. His method is to work back from the proclamation of Jesus' death and resurrection to find partial parallels and contrasts in the rich mythology of the Adam stories, about which he feels no obligation to be consistent or even particularly clear.

Paul's theology is unsystematic. We could go further and say that it is *deliberately* unsystematic. For, even in his own day, Paul would not allow his words to become the basis of a system. Critics tend to identify the opponents of Paul as 'conservative Jewish-Christians' or 'Hellenistic libertines', but probably the most persistently disruptive factor in Paul's career was the unwelcome enthusiasm of his own admirers, and the literalism with which they took his teaching. His letters are often designed to frustrate and infuriate them! The authenticity of the second letter to the Thessalonians is sometimes called into question because it is so different from and contradictory to the first letter.[3] But, surely, only Paul himself would have dared to be so perverse. Chance remarks of his in the first letter taken out of context had been used to show that 'the Day of the Lord had already come' (2 Thessalonians 2:2) and Paul has to disassociate himself from his own interpreters.

Similarly, in the Corinthian correspondence, Paul reserves his most vigorous sarcasm not for those who support the right of Peter or of Apollos to settle squabbles in the Church, but those who claim to belong to Paul (1 Corinthians 1:12f.). 'Was Paul crucified for you', he writes, 'or were you baptized in the name of Paul?' And he adds in the same ironic tone: 'I am thankful that I baptized none of you', with a few exceptions which truthfulness forces him to admit. In the following chapters, Paul launches into an attack on the wisdom of this world, particularly against those who looked up to him with excessive reverence and built out of his words a system of human wisdom. Paul cuts the ground from under their feet by claiming for his teaching no merit but the folly of the cross. Focusing on Paul's unwanted devotees rather than on his open adversaries helps us to explain the subsequent course of this correspondence.[4] For the argument is often directed against those who are trying to be more Pauline than Paul. He wants from his converts a true imitation of himself and not a parody. 'Give no offence to Jews or Gentiles or to the Church of God, just as I try to please all men in everything I do, not seeking my own advantage, but that of many, that they may be saved. So, be imitators of me, as I am of Christ' (1 Corinthians 10:32ff.).

I should want to claim, therefore, that Paul's letters cannot be scriptural because they preach one true doctrine of justification. The particular circumstances in which Paul wrote, the *ad hoc*, unsystematic character of his thought and his hostility towards the tendency, apparent even in his own day, to create a theological system out of his words, forbid any such conclusion.

Following on from this, I should also claim, that Paul's letters are not scripture because they represent the one and only authentic way of experiencing Christ. It may be the case that Paul himself 'experienced' justification, and felt an enormous sense of personal liberation from sin and guilt when he turned to Christ. If so, Paul makes strangely little of it in his letters. In fact, he seems to be uncertain about his own feelings and experiences, and even distances himself from them (2 Corinthians 12:2–4). Perhaps he recognized that he was not altogether typical as a follower of Jesus. Justification by faith is no better as a standard of religious experience than it is as a basis for theology. It may speak to us of the priority of God's grace and the freedom that is ours in Christ, and this truth may be appropriated in a brilliant moment of illumination and personal commitment. But a justified sinner has to learn first that his experience is not unique, others share it; nor is it invariable, other Christians do not have it. And he has to admit that he was, in a way, justified before he ever became aware of it, and remains still unjustified, in his own day-to-day experience afterwards. In other words, the believer may experience death and resurrection now, but only as an imperfect reflection of the death and resurrection of Jesus once for all, and of that future death and resurrection which await those who are in Christ. It is these emphatic past and future reference points in Paul's thinking that make this sort of interpretation of Paul ultimately unsatisfactory.

It appears that Paul's place in scripture is due neither to the truth of any theology we may try to construct around his words, nor to a prototype experience of encounter with Christ which can be presumed to lie behind them. The works of St Augustine or Luther or John Wesley are more theologically coherent and more luminous in their description of experience. But Paul is scripture and they are not. Is it then just an accident of historical priority, or is there some other more essential reason why the letters of Paul are included in the New Testament? The answer to this question which will emerge in the following section is that the presence of Paul's letters in scripture ensures the truth of the Incarnation of God's Word in Jesus Christ.

BELIEF IN THE BODY OF CHRIST

The letters of Paul speak of the reality and the 'incarnated-ness' of Christ's presence in the common life of Christians. Their limited and historical character, on this showing, far from disqualifying them as scripture, actually does the opposite. The more 'incarnate' they are in their own circumstances, the better they make their point. If we may refer again to that tiny epistle to Philemon as a test case for the scripturalness of Paul, it is in its concern with practical charity in one actual instance that it testifies to the Incarnation. A modern reader may feel a certain uneasiness that Paul does not take the opportunity to denounce the evils of slavery, and attack the economic structure of the Roman Empire which depended on that institution. But such theoretical denunciations would only divert attention away from the present reality of life in Christ. When Paul asks for the slave to be forgiven, he makes the appeal in this way: 'My brother, you owe me a favour in the Lord. Refresh my heart in Christ' (verse 20).

A constant and distinctive feature of Paul's language is his use of words like 'in Christ' or 'in the Lord' to summarize the meaning of salvation. The idiom recurs in many different contexts and has the function of linking what God has done through Christ and what Christians now are and do through him. Indeed, Paul describes members of the Church not as 'Christians' or as 'disciples' but as 'those who are in Christ'. Critics have found it difficult to account for this peculiar way of speaking. They have tried to explain it in various ways. It may be a kind of elliptical phrase for 'those who have been saved through Christ'. It may be that Christians are thought to belong to a new humanity derived from Christ, just as men are by nature derived from Adam and are literally *in* him, that is in the loins of their biological common ancestor. Alternatively, some have proposed that Paul conceives of Christ as a kind of mystical atmosphere which Christians breathe and live in. But the phrase defies logical analysis; it points towards a mystery of the incorporation of Christians into the person of Christ.[5]

The seeds of this idea were already sown in the teaching of Jesus. It is clear from Matthew 10:40, 'Whoever receives you receives me,' that Jesus adopted the Jewish institution of the 'business agent' or 'legal representative', the *shaliach*[6] (or apostle, as it is translated into Greek) and gave it a paradoxical twist. His surrogates were children, the poor and his own powerless little band of followers. Furthermore, Jesus' occasional use of Daniel's symbol of 'one like a Son of Man', to refer to the saints in their hope of vindication, contributes to the idea of a corporate or inclusive person.[7] In the light of the resurrection, the seeds germinate. Jesus' victory over death is already in a sense the vindication of the saints in him. He is the Son of Man. He is now represented on earth by his followers, who are one in him. This is not introduced by Paul as a theological theory, it is presented simply as a matter of fact, from which practical consequences flow.

A similar instance of incorporation language in Paul is the phrase 'the Body of Christ'. Again, this is a linking idea which can refer to the earthly Jesus and the body of the risen Christ, his presence in bread and wine at the Eucharist, and the community itself as the Body of Christ. Critics have traced partial similarities to the Stoic notion of man as a microcosm of the state, and more dubiously to pagan mythology concerning the body of the primal man.[8] Paul's image is unparalleled and distinctive of him, and yet it is nowhere presented as a theological novelty. It is employed by Paul in several places in 1 Corinthians as the basis of ethical exhortation. Christians are limbs in the Body of

Christ; they implicate him in what they do. So they must be holy and chaste (1 Corinthians 6:15). Christians, though many, are one body as they participate in the Eucharist (1 Corinthians 10:16). Therefore there must be no divisions between them, rich and poor, when they meet together (1 Corinthians 11:29, 33f.). Christians have different spiritual gifts, as they are different parts of the one Body of Christ (1 Corinthians 12:27). Those who do not speak in tongues are not to be despised, but given, if anything, greater honour. If we are right in attributing Colossians to Paul, it is clear that Paul can also conceive of the whole Church, made up of its dispersed communities, as one body over which Christ reigns as head (Colossians 1:18). In that letter Paul understands his own sufferings as 'a completion of what is lacking in Christ's afflictions, for the sake of his body that is the Church' (Colossians 1:24). At the same time as he speaks of Christ's transcendent sovereignty over the whole cosmos, Paul emphasizes the closeness of the association between Christ and the Church. 'In him the whole fulness of deity dwells bodily, and you have come to fulness of life in him' (Colossians 2:9f.). 'You have died, and your life is hid with Christ in God. When Christ who is our life appears, then you also will appear with him in glory' (Colossians 3:3f.).

Paul's language is puzzling and rather disturbing perhaps to us today. Although he always acknowledges the lordship of Jesus over his people, he often fails to make what we might think of as the proper distinction between Christ and the Church. I have tried to represent this ambiguity in the heading of this section. 'Belief in the Body of Christ' has two senses: that the Church is the place where belief is to be located, with the emphasis on the corporate and sacramental nature of faith; but also that belief can be directed towards the Church as its object. This is, of course, an article of the Creed: 'We believe in one, holy catholic and apostolic Church.' But we usually reconcile ourselves to this difficult idea, especially in the present divided state of the Christian churches, by treating this particular object of belief as a distant abstraction. So it is disconcerting to find Paul speaking of it in such a concrete way as the Body of Christ. For Paul, the Church is not an ideal floating somewhere above the actuality of his communities, which so conspicuously fail to match up to it. The Church as the Body of Christ is rather a real anticipation in the present of a future hope. As he says in Philippians 3:20, 'Our commonwealth is in heaven, and from it we await a Saviour, our Lord Jesus Christ, who will change our lowly body to be like his glorious body, by the power which enables him even to subject all things to himself.'

This brief discussion of Paul's language of salvation as incorporation into Christ through the Church may suffice to indicate how we understand Paul's letters as scripture. The New Testament canon does not end with the gospels' testimony to the fulfilment of God's promises to Israel in the coming of Christ, and to the Incarnation of God's Word in the person of Jesus. It is completed by the epistles of Paul, which witness to the continuing incarnation of Christ in the Church as a direct consequence of the Gospel. The risk which the Church ran in the writing down of the Gospel was that of producing a verbally disincarnate Christ. From the history of Christian theology it is clear how easily the Christ of the gospels can become the fleeting appearance of a religious ideal, or a phantom of historical reconstruction, detached from the living faith of the community. The significance of Paul in the New Testament is that he points to the sequel of the Incarnation, the community of faith as the Body of Christ.

THE CANONIZATION OF PAUL

We have seen that it is not Paul's rich and subtle theological mind nor his own vital experience of Christ that secures his place in Christian scripture. His letters are there because they testify to the continuing presence of the Word Incarnate in the corporate life of the Church. I have now to complete the picture by considering the remaining books in the New Testament canon. These, taken individually, appear to be an odd collection. The Acts of the Apostles, originally the companion volume to Luke's gospel, serves as a historical preface, describing the Church's missionary expansion during the first three decades. To the genuine letters of Paul have been added certain other works written under his name or later attributed to him. There are two letters of Peter, the second of which brings with it as a kind of echo the epistle of Jude, three letters of John and one of James. The collection is completed by the book of Revelation, which begins as though it were a series of apostolic letters addressed, like the Pauline corpus, to seven different destinations, but ends with a vision of hope for the future.

These writings have often been treated by biblical critics as secondary and inferior to the letters of Paul, as though they represented a decline from the pure inspiration of the apostle into more domestic issues of concern to the early Church. More recently, criticism has doubted whether it is correct to measure them against Paul in this way and has drawn attention to the wide diversity of the different currents in early Christian thought represented by this literature. Are these books, then, the frayed edges around the central unity of the New Testament canon? Or are they evidence for the view that there is only minimal unity in the New Testament, whose common denominator is no more than some kind of reference to Christ, and that the chief characteristic of the canon is its diversity?[9]

We shall argue that the function of the remainder of the canon is to provide a context for the proper understanding of Paul. Each of these writings in their various ways could be called 'deutero-Pauline', not in the sense that they fall away from Paul, but in the sense that they indicate how Paul is to be appreciated and understood by the Church. We might even argue that, without this literature, Paul's genuine letters would not have been admitted into the Christian canon of scripture. The only mention of the Pauline corpus in the New Testament is 2 Peter 3:13f. where, in the name of Peter, a hand of friendship is extended to Paul over the heads of those who had misinterpreted him. 'Our beloved brother Paul,' he says, 'writes according to the wisdom given to him, speaking of this [the hope for the Lord's return and the need to be prepared for it] as he does in all his letters.' The writer continues ominously: 'There are some things in them which are hard to understand, which the ignorant and unstable twist to their own destruction.' If it had not been for writings like 2 Peter the 'ignorant and unstable' might have had Paul to themselves and he would have been lost to the Church.

Let us begin with the material conventionally referred to as deutero-Pauline. The epistle to the Ephesians[10] may have been written by Paul with the assistance of a secretary, but it is more likely that it was composed as a kind of guide to the true understanding of Paul at the time when the surviving letters began circulating as a corpus. If so, it was, we should notice, intended to be read *alongside* the other letters and not instead of them. The author, who must have been a close student of Paul's own work, did not try to suppress or edit the genuine letters or comment directly upon them. He simply followed the Pauline precedent of letter-writing, and was thereby endorsing Paul's decision to choose this medium for the guidance of the Church, and encouraging his readers to go further and explore the rich variety of the apostle's writings. The emphasis in Ephesians on the universal and sacramental character of the Church is a development from what Paul had begun to say about the Body of Christ in Colossians. But there is an element of adaptation in response to the changed circumstances in which he was writing. Whereas Paul had claimed that Christ was the only foundation of the Church (1 Corinthians 3:11) the author, looking back to Paul, sees the Church as built on the apostles and prophets (Ephesians 2:20). But he is not, except in the trivial sense of modifying Paul's imagery, disagreeing with him. The highest position is still reserved for Christ, the chief cornerstone. For Ephesians as for Paul, Christ and the Church are one Body, and in the same way Gospel and apostle are one scriptural witness to the truth of the Incarnation.

By the time of Ephesians, perhaps between AD 80 and

90, it was no longer possible to believe, as Paul did, that the consummation of all things in Christ would take place before the end of one generation. And the author is silent on the subject of the second coming of Christ. But it is a diplomatic silence, not a theological one. He retains hope for the future in a quieter sense and does not deduce from the delay a revised understanding of salvation. The author asserts, more strongly perhaps than Paul, that Christians are already risen with Christ and seated in heaven (Ephesians 2:6), but he does not take this to imply that they are already perfectly enlightened and sinless. On the contrary, he stresses the need for perseverance and growth in the corporate life of the Church (Ephesians 4:15f.).

The pastoral epistles to Timothy and Titus are probably expansions by a later author of little personal notes from Paul originally similar to the letter to Philemon.[11] In the name of the apostle advice is here given on various practical concerns, such as the qualities necessary in candidates for the ministry, and the proper organization of charitable relief. It is easy to criticize them for trying to tame and domesticate Paul in a institutional setting which almost induces claustrophobia. But in their concern for the practical they are not essentially different from Paul himself, as 1 Corinthians in particular shows. The pastorals certainly lack Paul's sudden flashes of original insight and his brilliance of expression. They are content to appeal to 'sound doctrine' and 'the faith once delivered to the saints', which, they imply, is to be found by remaining obedient to the teaching of duly authorized leaders of the community. But it would be unfair to contrast their unadventurous conservatism with Paul's daring originality. For, like Paul himself, what they are opposed to is any attempt to create out of the apostle's theology a system which would threaten the truth of the Incarnation.

The author of the pastorals rejects Paulinism in the name of Paul. He rejects, for example, the system of Hymenaeus and Philetus (2 Timothy: 2:17f.) who 'have swerved from the truth by holding that the resurrection is past already'. The error of disincarnate, spiritualizing enthusiasm, which Paul had opposed already in Thessalonica and Corinth, was even more insidiously attractive to a later generation, trying to reconstruct Paul's teaching to cope with the delay in Christ's return. The present resurrection of the believer became for them, in contrast to the author of Ephesians, the basis for systematic exposition, or 'godless chatter and rotten talk' as the pastoral writer outspokenly dubs it. The writer's response to this threat is to insist on moral standards and loyalty to Church authorities. He refrains from answering the heretics with their own method, by giving an exegesis of Paul. In this sense, therefore, the pastoral epistles serve to canonize Paul; they refuse to allow his words to be twisted, or edited, or up-dated in a new theological system. Paul is simply to be received.

The letter to the Hebrews is an anonymous work, written a little after Paul's latest epistles, by someone who was acquainted with members of his circle. Yet it appears entirely free of influence from Paul's thought. It lacks any notion of incorporation into Christ. It is instead a rigorous exhortation against the danger of falling way from salvation already achieved. Hebrews is not deutero-Pauline in the sense that it was originally intended as a contribution to the debate about how Paul should be interpreted by the Church. But its eventual attribution to the apostle, accepted in the West by the end of the fourth century, made it, as it were, retrospectively deutero-Pauline. Its distinctiveness in comparison with the rest of the Pauline corpus continued to be acknowledged by its position in the canon after his other letters. The title by which it became known, 'To the Hebrews', is similarly a tacit recognition of its peculiarity; by implication this must have been what Paul wanted to say to his fellow Jews, while his other works were addressed to gentiles. Thus, to secure the canonization of the letter, the Church lent it the authority of Paul, but it also took steps to avoid any synthesis of its teachings with his. It stood rather as a testimony to the apostle's theological versatility, and showed that consistency with Pauline 'orthodoxy', if there were any such thing, is not a criterion of canonicity.

Hebrews also stands in the canon as a reminder that the Old Testament is the indispensable background for understanding the New Covenant.[12] The Jewish institutions of priesthood, sacrifice and Temple, which finally disappeared with the fall of Jerusalem in AD 70, were nevertheless continued and fulfilled in the person of Christ and in the Church's own corporate life. The continuing relevance of the Old Testament to Christian faith became a major issue in the interpretation of Paul in the post-apostolic age, and Hebrews made its special contribution to the outcome of that debate.

The remaining epistles of the New Testament, including the first three chapters of the book of Revelation, demonstrate the importance of the apostolic letter form for early Christian literature. They 'normalize' the letters of Paul by offering examples from other prominent leaders of the first generation: Peter, John and James. Critical study has cast doubt on the accuracy of these attributions, but the negative verdict on the question of authorship has a positive aspect, for it solves the problem of the conspicuous absence of detailed eye-witness testimony to the life of Jesus in works purporting to be written by those who knew him best.

The first letter of Peter is the work most strongly influenced by Paul's thought and language; it is not, however, an exercise in theological construction, but a moving exhortation to martyrdom. The epistle of James has a similarly ethical stress in less threatening circumstances, and warns against the mistake of drawing false conclusions from the language of justification by faith. His assertion that 'a man is justified by works and not by faith alone' (James 2:24) is so starkly contradictory that Paulinists have always been tempted to edge the epistle out of the canon altogether. But clearly the author is not attacking Paul, he is opposing misapplications of Paul's words in a situation completely different from that of Galatians and Romans. Both 1 Peter and James, in their own ways, contribute to the canonization of Paul. They show how he is to be applied, and how he is not to be applied, to the changing situation of the community.

The apostolic letter becomes a norm not only for works that were to be included in the canon, but also for the pastoral letters of bishops like Clement of Rome and Ignatius of Antioch,[13] and the encyclicals of their successors. This form of communication acts as a reminder that Christian truth cannot be detached from the living structure of the community which perceives it. For it is always incarnate, contextualized and embodied.

The insistence on the continuing life of the Church in the world explains another feature which is prominent in several of the works we have been considering, and which is given its fullest scope in the book of Revelation: that is hope for the future. In the post-apostolic age, as hope for the imminent return of Christ seemed to be disappointed, it was tempting to discard it, or translate it into non-temporal, purely spiritual form. But the temptation is resisted strongly. The original expectations of Jesus and the first generation are allowed to stand in the gospels and in the epistles of Paul. Certain aspects of future hope are admittedly interpreted to apply to life here and now, on this side of the end of the world, as they were already by Paul and by Jesus himself. But these reinterpretations are placed with apparent inconsistency alongside the literal hope. For the Church realized that to abandon the future dimension was also to abandon the historical dimension and therefore the reality of the Incarnation.

Finally, let us consider the Acts of the Apostles, and take up first the point we have just made. Some recent studies of Luke-Acts have suggested that this work is exceptional in the New Testament in that it has pushed expectation of the End so far into the distant future as to make it inoperative as a force in the present.[14] This is not, however, borne out by the evidence. In Luke's gospel, as in the others, future hope and present realization appear side by side. And it is a mistake to think of the Acts of the Apostles as an instance of the Church settling down comfortably for a long wait, musing on its own past and organizing its institutional life. If Acts was written around AD 100, it is not a history of the Church to date, but the account of a limited and particularly important section of that history, in which the Gospel was taken from Jerusalem to Rome. On Luke's understanding, the End could not have arrived before that mission was completed and all men offered the chance to hear the message of salvation. But, like his contemporaries, he left open the question of how much longer the world was going to last.

Luke-Acts[15] links together the Gospel and the apostolic witness to it in an inseparable unity, and concentrates in its second volume on the figures of Peter and John, James the Lord's brother, and above all Paul. It thus provides the structure for the New Testament canon itself, gospels and epistles, chiefly of Paul but of others also. It is significant that Acts does not even mention the fact that Paul wrote letters. For it is not interested in portraying Paul as the architect of a theological system.[16] The speeches in Acts are made to fit their differing contexts, rather than the differing identities of the speakers. When faint echoes of Paul's distinctive ideas do appear (as in Acts 10:24ff. and 15:7—11), it is Peter not Paul who is given them to say. Paul's significance for Luke does not lie in his theology, but in his missionary achievement. In co-operation with the other apostles, he made the Way of Jesus truly universal and catholic.

In this chapter I posed the question of why the New Testament contains writings in addition to the four gospels. And I suggested that Paul's epistles, which form the core of the second half of the canon, function not as a standard of doctrine, but as witness to the Incarnation in the corporate experience of the Church. The role of the other literature is to protect Paul from Paulinizing misinterpretation and to allow his witness to be heard. On this view, the unity of the New Testament is secure, however much biblical criticism may want to emphasize, in the main rightly, the wide diversity of theological opinion among the writers. The structure of the New Testament canon points towards the life of the Body of Christ in the world as the context for its proper understanding, and at the same time invites, even necessitates, critical and historical inquiry. Scripture is both the fountain and the well of truth, and the excavation of the well by the methods of criticism releases the same living water which flows in a continuous stream through the tradition and corporate life of the Church.

FURTHER READING

H. J. Richards, *St Paul and his Epistles*, DLT, 1980
   A popular, critical introduction.
K. Stendahl, *Paul among Jews and Gentiles*, SCM 1977
   This scholar criticizes the dogmatic and unhistorical treatment of Paul in his own Lutheran tradition.
D. E. Whiteley, *The Theology of St Paul*, Basil Blackwell, 1975
   Despite his systematic arrangement of topics, this is the best treatment of Paul's thought in English.

5   A Biblical Agenda

LIMITATIONS

In the last three chapters I have tried to trace an outline of
the shape and unity of the Bible, broadly consistent with
both the findings of criticism and the faith of the Church.
The Bible does not underestimate the transcendence of
God or the ambiguity of human experience. In this it
simply reflects the world as we experience it. But the Bible
witnesses, nonetheless, to a hope which came to fulfilment
in Jesus. The ultimate purpose of all creation, God's Word,
is expressed in his words, his life story and his person; and
the salvation he brings is communicated through the consequence of the Incarnation of the Word, the Church as the
Body of Christ. It remains in this last chapter to draw out
some of the practical implications of what we have said for
the Church's use of the Bible today.

The first item on any agenda is likely to be 'apologies
for absence', and that is also appropriate here. It would
not have been possible in such a small volume to give even
the shortest summary of the theology and ethics of the
biblical literature; and to have attempted it would have
given a false impression of the unity which properly belongs
to scripture. The Bible has many different things to say
about God and about the good life for man, which are
worthy of separate and detailed treatment. But neither the
individual books nor the canon of scripture as a whole
presents a single theological or ethical system. As we have
seen, this is not even the case with the letters of Paul,
much less with the other parts of scripture. For the sake

of intellectual tidiness, philosophical theologians have in the course of Christian history made several attempts to weave the threads of the Bible into systems of this kind, but the best of them have always admitted, what their followers have often forgotten, that the truth is larger than our capacity to perceive it at any particular moment. A theory, however brilliant, is no substitute for the reality it seeks to understand. And some theories, by their very brilliance, induce the sort of trance that anaesthetizes us against reality. By contrast, the Bible is more true to life. It presents us with truth incarnate: the mystery and the realism of the Incarnation, which is understood only partially even by the Church, and cannot be apprehended except by incorporation into it. Paul expresses this point himself in a typically vivid contrast: 'Now we see in a mirror dimly, then face to face' (1 Corinthians 13:12). 'And we all with faces unveiled, behold as in a mirror the glory of the Lord, and are already being changed into his likeness from one degree of glory to another' (2 Corinthians 3:18).

Under the heading of practical agenda, we might be expected to refer to the ethics of the Bible, but we offer instead our apologies. We cannot discuss here the way the Church ought to use the Bible in relation to the issues which confront the world today: pacificism, racism, conservation, sexual ethics, unemployment, the rights of women, poverty in the third world, and so forth.[1] This is not because the Bible has nothing to say to us on these matters, even less because they are unimportant. It is because no simple solutions can ever be conjured out of ancient texts to problems which belong to a world organized in a way utterly different from that of the Bible. What scripture has to contribute to such discussions is chiefly the advice, implied by its own example, that we must begin where we are, incarnated in our own situation.

When we look at what the Bible does say in detail on matters of social and personal ethics, we are at first struck by its illiberal tone and its lack of tolerance; this can be a salutary lesson, if it forces us to re-examine the basis of our own liberalism. It is not only the Bible, but the modern world as well, which is culturally conditioned and relative. By its capacity to affront the received wisdom of our age, the Bible adds a new dimension, creating the possibility of real dialogue. It is too easy, and in any case critically unjustified, for the Church to retreat on to the safe ground of a few liberal-sounding texts, and try to claim that this is what the Bible really has to say to us today. Such a use of the Bible confirms our own prejudices, is insufficiently specific to solve our problems, and can quickly back-fire as an attempt to promote the moral authority of scripture. Christians understandably treasure the words of Jesus on the love of enemies or the infinite possibility of forgiveness, but they are not thereby entitled to neglect his stern warnings of God's future judgement and the threat of punishment. The liberal intolerance and humane rigorism of the historical Jesus remain an enigma until they are appropriated in a community which possesses the Spirit and mind of Christ. Biblical criticism and Christian faith in the Incarnation are united in their opposition to any attempt to abstract ethical ideals from scripture and throw the rest away.

It is, on the other hand, important for the Church not to over-react to the discovery that the Bible is ethically varied, inconsistent and conditioned by historical circumstances. This does not mean that we should cease to use it in our discussions of ethics, or abandon the one emphasis on which scripture is uniformly agreed (the necessity of obedience to the will of God) and substitute instead the uncertain inner light of moral reason. The Church has the right, which perhaps it ought to enforce more strongly than it currently does, to regulate the behaviour of its members. And Christians are under obligation to obey the Law of Christ, which is indeed the law of their own new life in him.

I must also apologize for what must seem an even more serious absence, my failure to give proper consideration to the theology of the Bible. But the diversity of theological views implied in scripture defies brief description or easy synthesis.[2] There is a kind of family resemblance between them, of course, but if we try to distil out what they all have in common, the result is very thin milk. The theologies of the Bible stand in a dialectical relation to each other. They represent a series of contrasting truths; in the Old Testament, for instance, between Law and Wisdom, or between prophecy and apocalyptic; in the New Testament between the present and future Kingdom of God, or the earthly Jesus and the risen Christ. The synthesis which later Christian theology has struggled towards is not a matter of conflating the biblical material and reducing it to essentials, but of holding its truths together in balance and understanding it as a whole.

It may appear deeply unsatisfactory that we are unable to construct a coherent theology on the basis of the Bible alone, and to state its truth in a set of theological propositions, denial of which would then constitute heresy. But critical study and our experience within the believing community force us to admit the pluralism of scripture, and sometimes the equal validity of differing interpretations of it. This does not at all imply that we should adopt a *laissez faire* attitude towards blatant distortions of Christian truth. The Bible does impose limits on what we ought to believe, chiefly the limit imposed by the need to accept the Bible as a whole. Heresy in its classic forms and in its modern disguises usually involves not the rejection of the Bible, but the partial and exaggerated acceptance of one element of scripture above the rest. We may doubt whether today ecclesiastical discipline is the best way of dealing with the problem, but the Church has the duty to recall its members to the wholeness of the truth revealed in scripture, and to insist on commitment to its worship and corporate life as the practical test of right belief.

The topics I wish to place on our agenda instead are more limited in scope, but still far too large to handle in anything but a preliminary way. They are the use of the Bible in prayer, in liturgy and in the renewal of the Church.

91

THE BIBLE AND SPIRITUALITY

Private reading of scripture in the context of prayer is a practice now common to Christians whatever their denomination. The monastic tradition of spiritual reading (*lectio divina*),[3] the invention of printing and the spread of literacy, the primacy of scripture in reforms of the Church, and the concentration on biblical studies in institutions which train the clergy: all these in their different ways contributed to this modern phenomenon. There was a time when the Roman Catholic laity were discouraged from imitating their Protestant brethren in devotional reading of the Bible, but that is no longer so. The Second Vatican Council 'earnestly and specifically urges all the Christian faithful . . . to learn by frequent reading of the divine scriptures the "excelling knowledge of Jesus Christ" (Philippians 3:8). "For ignorance of the Scriptures is ignorance of Christ" (St Jerome).'[4]

It is necessary to warn against certain dangers in this practice. First, there is the risk of what we might call, rather crudely, spiritual narcissism. We come to prayer full of our own troubles and desires, in search of help and guidance. If we approach the Bible in the same way the temptation is either to make the portion of text we happen to be reading say what we want to hear, or else we fly to those favourite verses which we know have the effect of reassuring or comforting us. Scripture then loses its capacity to speak to us and becomes just another instance of the eccentric and disturbing habit of speaking to oneself. Second, there is the danger of supposing that the meaning of scripture is always self-evident, so that anyone, however uninformed, can achieve instant comprehension. We naturally want to distinguish between spiritual reading and historical research, but to rely on intuitive guesswork about straightforward factual details is not only foolish, it is spiritually arrogant. The pure word of God which the believer is trying to hear should not be confused with a pure, unmarked edition of the biblical text. A modern translation with annotations, or the notes published, for

92

example, by the Bible Reading Fellowship are an obvious and necessary precaution against gross error and flights of fancy.[5] Third, there is the danger of isolationism, the risk of taking the primary reference of scripture to be the relation between God and the individual soul. The private reading of scripture may even lead to a 'privatization' of religion, and its reduction to 'what a man does with his solitude'.[6] On this view, the reality of other people's experience and of the external world of space and time become secondary and almost illusory.

All of these dangers come round in the end to a denial of the incarnate and corporate character of biblical truth. Christians never can read the Bible entirely on their own. Even when they are alone, they remain integrally connected with the other members of Christ's Body, and spiritual reading is an extension and deepening of corporate reading. It is only in this context that much of the Bible really makes any sense, for this book is, as it were, the family album of the people of God. Along with the record of those crucial events which mark the turning points in their history, there are also some curious souvenirs picked up on pilgrimage, some dark corners and shady characters. But the Christian reader cannot ultimately disown any of it. We know who we are, because we identify with this book, and own it as our past. The difficulties which the ordinary reader frequently encounters in scripture usually arise from forgetting the corporate nature of salvation. God chooses first of all a people for his own possession, and he addresses and calls individuals in so far as they belong to that people. This was true of Israel, but it remains equally true with the coming of Christ, through whom all men and women now become God's chosen race. If a particular passage does not seem to have any relevance to our condition, we should look up and recall the people to which we belong. The distance and strangeness of scripture, which criticism emphasizes, are essential features of it. We discover our real selves in our past precisely by respecting its difference from the present. As individuals we scan our own personal history, and remember in penitence what it was really like, and not what we would prefer to believe about it. The people of God find their identity by being taken out of the present into their initially strange and different past.

The corporate life of the Church is founded on the person of Christ, and a corporate reading of scripture is, therefore, also a Christ-centred or christological reading. The Bible is a book about the word of God made flesh in Christ. It is a portrait of Jesus surrounded by a frame, a very large frame admittedly, and heavily gilded in places. But, surprisingly, it does not swamp the delicate miniature of the gospels. The opposite is the case. The picture of Christ there expands to fill the frame. For the earthly Jesus is one with the eternal Word who made the heavens and directs the life of men towards God. When Christians read the Old Testament christologically, as we argued in our second chapter, they are not attributing to its authors conscious and precise foreknowledge of later history. If they had possessed such amazing prescience, their words would have had little point or contemporary relevance in their own contexts. It is more often the gaps and the inconclusiveness of what is said in the Old Testament that point to Christ as its fulfilment. Christians may discern types of Christ as they read of Adam or Isaac, Joshua or David, but these figures are also antitypes to him, and they have a separate function and a place of their own. The form which Christ takes in the reading of scripture is often implicit and anonymous. Wherever Israel in the wilderness thirsts for the living God, she discovers the rock, which is Christ, from which life-giving water can be struck (1 Corinthians 10:4).

The corporate and christological reading of scripture is also 'spiritual' reading in the sense that it involves encounter with the Spirit of God, who spoke through the prophets and is present in the believing community as the Spirit of the risen Christ. Christians believe that the Holy Spirit inspires both the writing and the reading of scripture; he is the hidden author and interpreter of the Bible. What does this mean? Certainly not that the Bible is factually inerrant. For the Spirit co-operates with the humanity of the authors, he does not annihilate it. Nor does it mean that the reader is permitted to ignore the literal meaning and superimpose clever constructions of his own. The inspiration of the biblical writers is more like the 'inspiration' of a work of art, whereby words intended for one generation manage to cross the barriers of time and culture and speak effectively to men and women of a later age. The explanation of the 'universal' quality of scripture is not, or not often, to be found in the literary artistry of the writers but in the realism and authenticity of their encounter with God. The inspiration of the readers of the Bible is the God-given insight into its hidden meaning for faith. The 'second meaning' of scripture is chiefly the second meaning of love. As St John Chrysostom said, describing scripture as a whole as a letter from God: 'When we receive a letter we pay attention not only to the contents of it but also the affection of the writer expressed in it.' As the Christian reads the Bible in prayer, he or she begins to sense the love of God between the lines — the love that is a consuming fire of judgement upon us, and at the same time the source of light and the saving power of grace.

These are the guidelines, then, which our study has suggested for the use of the Bible in Christian prayer: scripture is to be read corporately as the life-history of the people of God; christologically, as witness to the Word Incarnate; and spiritually, as the means by which the Holy Spirit reveals the reality and love of God. These are, of course, not alternative approaches to scripture, but different facets of the Christian way of understanding the wholeness of biblical truth.[7]

THE BIBLE AND LITURGY

The worship of almost all Christian denominations today is increasingly centred on the Eucharist and the sacrament of holy communion. Protestants are rediscovering this key element of their faith, obscured in the past by reaction to popular abuses and theological controversies with Roman

Catholicism. Catholics no longer allow the Mass to be used as a private devotion for priests, and have re-emphasized it as their central act of worship, in which the people themselves participate fully, in a language they understand. The modern 'eucharistic revolution' has had a profound effect on the Church's use of scripture. It has located the ministry of the word firmly in a sacramental context which brings out its corporate character. Revised lectionaries have corrected the imbalance of reading the New Testament in isolation at the Eucharist, by providing for an Old Testament lesson and a psalm alongside the epistle and the gospel. The Sunday texts are arranged according to a consistent theme, and the choice of readings is influenced to some extent by the findings of scholarly criticism. The variety of the scriptural witness is reflected in the use of two or three year cycles, which lessens the danger of elevating one set of passages permanently above the rest of scripture, and treating them as a fixed and invariable statement of Christian truth. The placing of the sermon in the Eucharist after the proclamation of the gospel and before the recitation of the Creed has purified our understanding of preaching in worship, and made it more biblical and doctrinal.

These changes are by and large welcome improvements. But there are some disadvantages which we should be aware of and take measures to correct. The time available for public reading of scripture in normal Sunday worship, and the internal pace and rhythm of the liturgy, mean that only short passages can be used. The New Testament suffers from this treatment. But the Old Testament is totally misrepresented by short snippets from the better known stories, purple passages from the prophets and a few verses from the longer psalms. There is little opportunity to grasp the larger context or linger over the meaning for faith of the text that is actually being read. The designated theme can become more important than the readings, and when this happens the vivid and concrete character of the Bible is sacrificed to an abstraction. The homily at the Eucharist has to conform to the dynamics of the liturgy, and therefore cannot include detailed exposition of the texts for their own sake.

With the rise of the Eucharist as the principal Sunday service in the Anglican Church, there has been an inevitable decline in the office as a form of public worship. The traditional offices still play a significant part in the spiritual discipline of the clergy, and in the worship of 'specialist centres' like cathedrals, monastic communities and educational institutions. But if scripture is to have its proper place in the liturgy, we need to discover new ways of enriching the ministry of the word at the level of the local congregation.

In former times, preparation for communion was largely a matter of private examination of conscience and perhaps going to confession. The Church today is gradually recognizing that the community no less than the individual believer needs to be prepared, and that this should include corporate reading and meditation on the biblical texts that are to be used in the Eucharist, as well as a corporate expression of penance and reconciliation. There is room for a variety of forms here, involving the whole congregation, smaller groups, or even the members of a single family.[8] The leaders of the local community, both ordained and lay, need to be flexible enough to facilitate and encourage, rather than to dominate, this process of corporate preparation. Those who are to preach the word in the Eucharist must first hear the word addressed to and present within the community. They need themselves to listen and to learn, if liturgical preaching is to be a genuine act of corporate worship.[9]

At certain points in the year, it should be possible for the community to experiment with more patient exercises in the corporate reading of scripture: parish retreats, for example, or a longer ministry of the word in Advent or Lent, and above all during Holy Week and Easter. To do justice to the character of scripture itself, corporate reading should not be allowed to become too cerebral or academic. The message of a biblical text can sometimes best be appreciated through music and the visual arts, or through dramatic representation. The prime example of this already is the symbolic action of the Eucharist, and that ought to provide the encouragement to explore other possibilities with imagination and daring. The proclamation of scripture in worship should be an experience which touches all the senses and the different capacities of the whole community, children as well as adults, the practical-minded as well as the more intellectual, the charismatic as well as those of a more reserved disposition.[10]

It is not my purpose here to advance a detailed programme for change in the Church's liturgical use of scripture. Different local communities will feel the need for change in varying degrees, and will have different resources on hand to meet it. I am more concerned with the principle which has emerged from our study, that the Word of God is not heard if it is merely verbal; it has to become incarnate in the corporate life and worship of the believing community. It would be a tragedy if the renewed emphasis on the Eucharist should lead to a neglect of scripture or a separation of word and sacrament. The two belong together. The sacramental context of the Church's use of scripture ensures that the Bible will be correctly understood.[11] But it is equally true to say that the scriptural context of the Church's worship ensures that the Eucharist will be properly understood, not as mere ceremonial but as the celebration of life. For it is the Bible which directs the sacrament towards its ultimate reality, Jesus as the Word of God made flesh for our salvation, and the offering of the whole of life as the community's response to God's grace.

THE BIBLE AND RENEWAL

The third item on our agenda is what would once have been called the reformation of the Church, but is now less polemically referred to as renewal. I want to argue that it is the rediscovery of the Bible by Christianity today which is the major stimulus towards renewal. As illustrations of this I shall mention briefly the issues of secularization and ecumenism. These are the two most striking phenomena in twentieth-century Church history and their relation to the Bible and the Christian faith has often been misunderstood.

Secular opponents of the Church long ago predicted its imminent collapse under the weight of historical and scientific criticism, and are now scarcely able to conceal their astonishment that it has managed to survive at all into the modern world. Religion, they believed, was set on a course of inexorable decline in contemporary society. What they failed to reckon with was that the Church itself would actually participate in the process of secularization, and welcome it as a consequence of fidelity to scripture. In response to the Bible's emphasis on the autonomy of creation and the significance of history, and above all as a direct result of belief in the Incarnation, the Church has been turning more and more outwards towards the world, and has positively revalued the secular. The gradual dismantling of the religious establishment, together with other forms of secularization in Western society, has served to reinvigorate Christianity and restore its peculiar power. For the type of religious faith to which men and women today are likely to be drawn is one which takes the secular structures of ordinary life seriously, as perhaps only the religion of the Incarnation can.

The ecumenical movement was once thought to be clear evidence that the end of the Church was near: the old denominations were trying to cover up their weakness and failure by banding together. According to one sociologist of religion 'organizations amalgamate when they are weak, rather than when they are strong, since alliance means compromise and amendment of commitment.'[12] But this is dubious as a generalization, when applied, for example, in the fields of trade union politics or international trade, and it is particularly misleading when applied to ecumenism. Unity schemes this century have spectacularly flopped when they have been felt to offer merely financial or organizational benefits at the expense of principle. But, on the other hand, there have been sudden unexpected advances in the cause of Christian unity, not least in areas of the world where the Church was expanding rapidly.

The comparatively speaking stronger parties to ecumenical dialogue have frequently made what could be taken as 'unforced concessions'. The Protestant denominations in the World Council of Churches seem to have found a new regard for Church tradition, for the social dimension of religion and even for the pastoral office of a bishop. The Roman Catholic Church, on its own initiative, has re-examined its structures and its whole ethos, carrying through reforms with the speed and almost total unanimity of which only such a highly disciplined body is capable. Far from constituting an amendment of commitment, for many Christians the ecumenical movement has been a challenge to greater commitment to the one Lord, and to the biblical emphasis on the unity of his earthly Body. Nevertheless, the Church's renewed concern for the secular and for the ecumenical can still be misconstrued, even by believers, as the acquiescence and tolerance which are akin to doubt, unless its basis in the Bible and Christian theology are made clearer; and this remains on our current agenda.

The churches are beginning to submit their peculiar past histories and their present forms of worship and life to the test of scripture. This does not mean that they are attempting to turn the clock back to the first century; the problem of 'cultural relativism' is much more widely appreciated than some biblical critics suppose. Nor does it mean that they are denying the continuity of tradition; the importance of tradition is increasingly stressed. It is more a case of acknowledging, what the Bible already strongly attests, that the people of God are not exempt from the risk of falling away into hardness of heart and contempt for his word and commandments. The ecumenical movement is an act of corporate penitence.

When the Bible is used to reform the Church, it is not being assumed that the stream is purest at its source. It is rather that impurities are more conspicuous and intolerable there. As it follows its course, the river of faith has filtered out some impurities and picked up others, and sometimes insidiously diluted them and conditioned its users to tolerate a high level of contamination. The water of which the Bible is the fountain and well is living water only when it runs freely into the present and surges towards the future. The use of the Bible in the renewal of the Church is to help to eliminate the dirt and debris, and to let the water flow.

The churches have the Bible in common. It is the chief and even unique distinguishing mark that makes a community recognizable as a Christian church. But in another sense there will not be a common Bible until there is a common Church. For mere possession of this literature is, as we have seen, not enough. It is the understanding and appropriation of the Bible in a particular way which makes it constitutive of the Church. And the existence of one reconciled and reintegrated Body of Christ is essential to the unity of scripture. The context of interpretation is all-important. Take as just one example the words of John the Baptist in John 1:29, 'Behold the Lamb of God, who takes away the sins of the world.' They have a completely different meaning when they are emblazoned over the head of the Rev Ian Paisley on a fund-raising tour for Ulster loyalists,[13] or are used as the invitation to communion at the Catholic mass which he so fiercely abominates. And the difference between a certain kind of Protestant atonement theology and Catholic sacramentalism is not an academic one in the context of Northern Ireland. This is simply the most extreme example of what I mean when I say that the recovery of the oneness of the Church and the oneness of scripture are inseparable objectives for Christians today.

ANY OTHER BUSINESS?

The end of an agenda is often an anti-climax. It is an open invitation to the talkative, amid mounting irritation from the rest, to drag the proceedings out with a miscellany of unanswered questions. But the Church is not, please God, an interminable committee, but a body of men and women with a commission and with urgent business to attend to elsewhere. A discussion like ours, on how the Bible is to be used in the Church, should end with the business of actually being the Church and using it.

What we need first for the future is not less, but more and better criticism. We are entitled to expect from biblical scholars that their method, which prides itself on its objectivity, will eventually produce clear results and a critical consensus. In some respects it already has, but in others there is still too much confusion and controversy. Scientific enquiry thrives on unrestricted debate, and its freedom to engage in this should be respected. But critical freedom ought to be differentiated sharply from the licence to indulge in personal idiosyncracy and careerism. Biblical scholars have their work cut out if they are to reach down into the depths of the well and convince each other about what is there to be discovered. They are human after all, and if they are to find the truth in the well of scripture, and not a pale reflection of their own faces, they need to remember the lessons of humility and complete honesty with themselves which faith teaches. A certain measure of blame for the inattentiveness of the Church to what they have said in the past must rest with them. Let them say it again more clearly and more convincingly, for the Church needs to hear it.

Equally, the Church has work to do with the Bible, especially perhaps in the areas we have mentioned in this chapter. All our attempts at modernization of the forms of prayer, worship and Church life will simply result in a superficial and impoverished version of Christian faith, unless we are ready at the same time to be grasped afresh by its hidden power, which the Bible, as the fountain of truth, enables us to identify as the living Christ. Ministers and clergy have a special responsibility to provide against this danger of famine in the modern Church, 'not a famine of bread nor a thirst for water, but of hearing the words of the Lord' (Amos 8:11). Through intellectual laziness and fear of disturbing the institution, they have often allowed themselves to slide, either into a naive biblical fundamentalism, or into a kind of mechanical sacramentalism, and have defended themselves in both cases on the grounds of pastoral considerations. But they, above all, ought to know that faith in Christ is not a soothing falsehood but the most realistic of creeds, and that critical reason and living tradition are not irreconcilable opposites, but complementary means of perceiving the truth. We have a right to expect them to share this knowledge with us through their preaching and teaching.

It only remains on this agenda to fix a date for the next meeting. There is reason to hope that it will be unnecessary for anyone to attempt to write a book like this in AD 2033, which will be the second centenary of the Oxford Movement. The Church may even have so moved on to other things by then, that it will see no special reason to mark that anniversary. That will be all to the good, if it means that the one truth of scripture, and the integrity of faith and criticism are by then simply common assumptions, universally held in the one Church of Jesus Christ.

FURTHER READING

R. E. Brown, *Biblical Reflections on Crises facing the Church*, Chapman, 1975
This shows how biblical criticism may be used in practical concerns of the Church today.

J. N. M. Wijngaards, *Communicating the Word of God*, Mayhew-McCrimmon, 1978
An imaginative approach to the task of communicating to Church people the message of the Bible.

For other works on Bible study and preaching see the notes to this chapter.

General Reading

Illustrated descriptions of the world of ancient Israel and the New Testament are perhaps the easiest way into biblical study for the general reader:

B. W. Anderson, *The Living World of the Old Testament*, Longmans, 3rd edn., 1978

H. C. Kee and F. W. Young, *The Living World of the New Testament*, Prentice Hall, 1980

One-volume Bible commentaries, though expensive, provide scholarly discussion of general issues as well as detailed comment on the text. The best are:

M. Black and H. H. Rowley (eds.), *Peake's Commentary on the Bible*, Nelson, 1963

R. E. Brown, J. A. Fitzmyer and R. Murphy (eds.), *The Jerome Biblical Commentary*, Chapman, 1968

Short summaries of recent biblical scholarship are:

R. E. Clements, *A Century of Old Testament Study*, Lutterworth, 1976

R. H. Fuller, *The New Testament in Current Study*, SCM, 1962

Spiritual meditations on biblical themes are largely a matter of personal taste. I especially like:

U. Simon, *Story and Faith*, SPCK, 1975
L. Santucci, *Wrestling with Christ*, Collins, 1972

Two recent books which discuss the question of what the Old and New Testaments mean as a whole are:

B. S. Childs, *Introduction to the Old Testament as Scripture*, SCM, 1979

J. D. G. Dunn, *Unity and Diversity in the New Testament*, SCM, 1977

The best discussion of the history of the canon is:

H. von Campenhausen, *The Formation of the Christian Bible*, A. & C. Black, 1972

Older but still invaluable books, written from within the tradition of the Oxford Movement, and providing the classic Catholic Anglican understanding of scripture, are:

A. G. Hebert, *The Authority of the Old Testament*, Faber, 1947
A. M. Ramsey, *The Gospel and the Catholic Church*, Longmans, 2nd edn., 1956

Notes

CHAPTER 1 *Christian Faith and Biblical Criticism*

1 See above, the books listed for General Reading.

2 As D. E. Nineham, *The Use and Abuse of the Bible*, Macmillan, 1976.

3 *The First Book of Homilies*, SPCK edn., 1908.

4 John 4:4–15 in James Moffatt's translation.

5 Palestinian Targum on Genesis 28:10; see R. E. Brown, *The Gospel According to John I-XII*, Anchor Bible, Chapman, 1966, p. 170f.

6 Compare Origen's allegory on the text of Numbers 21:16, 'Spring up, O well, the well which kings have dug': 'That which we now have in our hands, which has been read to us, is a well, and so are all the Scriptures of the Law and the Prophets; so all the evangelical and apostolic writings are one well, which none can dig or delve except they be kings and princes. Truly kings and princes are they who remove the earth from the well, remove the surface-meaning of the letter, and from the rock within, from where Christ is, bring forth the spiritual meanings as living water.' *Homily on Numbers*, Migne, P. G. xii, p. 658. Needless to say, the analogy is used rather differently here.

7 For a discussion of this see C. F. Evans, *Is Holy Scripture Christian?*, SCM, 1971.

8 Speaking against contentious opponents, who enjoyed arguments about what is really scripture, *To the Philadelphians*, 8.

9 See K. Rahner and C. Ernst, *Sacramentum Mundi*, vol. 6, Burns and Oates, 1970, pp. 54–7.

10 P. C. Rodger and L. Vischer (eds), *The Fourth World Conference on Faith and Order*, SCM, 1964, p. 50.

11 W. M. Abbott (ed.), *The Documents of Vatican II*, Chapman, 1966, p. 117.

12 See A. E. Harvey (ed.), *God Incarnate, Story and Belief*, SPCK, 1981, ch. 1.

13 See P. Stuhlmacher, *Historical Criticism and Theological Interpretation of Scripture*, SPCK, 1979.
14 Compare, e.g., Exodus 6:3 with Genesis 15:7.
15 See S. L. Greenslade (ed.), *The Cambridge History of the Bible*, Cambridge University Press, vol. 3, 1963, chs. 7 and 8.
16 As G. Faber aptly called them, *Oxford Apostles*, Faber, 1933.
17 *The Reconstruction of Belief*, John Murray, 1926, p. 973, my emphasis.

CHAPTER 2 *Images of Hope*

1 See C. S. Lewis, *Reflections on the Psalms*, Bles, 1958.
2 Jesus refers to the first and last martyrs, Abel (Genesis 4:10) and Zechariah (2 Chronicles 24:21) in the order of their appearance in the Hebrew canon, Matthew 23:35.
3 In the discussion of the identity of John the Baptist as the returning Elijah, Mark 9:11.
4 E.g., 'Each day has troubles enough of its own,' Matthew 6:34; and 'The poor you have always with you,' Mark 14:7.
5 See G. Vermes, *The Dead Sea Scrolls in English*, Penguin Books, 2nd edn., 1975.
6 See P. R. Ackroyd and C. F. Evans (eds), *The Cambrdige History of the Bible*, vol. 1, Cambridge University Press, 1970, chs 8 and 12.
7 E.g., H. Ringgren, *Israelite Religion*, SPCK, 1966.
8 W. Eichrodt, *Theology of the Old Testament*, SCM, vol. 1, 1960; vol. 2, 1967.
9 G. von Rad, *Old Testament Theology*, Oliver and Boyd, 1962.
10 The approaches of Eichrodt and von Rad are compared by D. Spriggs, *Two Old Testament Theologies*, SCM, 1974.
11 See further B. S. Childs, *Exodus*, SCM, 1974, p. 47ff.
12 E.g., Psalm 74 and Isaiah 51:9—11.
13 SCM Press, 1954, p. 43f.
14 Compare Ezra 3:10—13.
15 See E. W. Nicholson, *Exodus and Sinai in History and Tradition*, Basil Blackwell, 1973.
16 See C. F. D. Moule (ed.), *The Significance of the Resurrection for Faith in Jesus Christ*, SCM, 1968.
17 In the Apocrypha, 2 Esdras: 3—14 (or 4 Ezra).
18 The text may be found in R. H. Charles, *Apocrypha and Pseudepigrapha of the Old Testament*, vol. 2, Oxford University Press, 1913.
19 See O. Kaiser, *Isaiah 1—12*, SCM, 1972, p. 96ff.

20 See H. H. Rowley, *Worship in Ancient Israel*, SPCK, 1967.
21 See W. Foerster, *From Exile to Christ*, Fortress Press, 1964.
22 See J. Bowker, *Problems of Suffering in Religions of the World*, Cambridge University Press, 1970.
23 For a selection of different translations see H. H. Rowley, *From Moses to Qumran*, Lutterworth, 1963, p. 180, n. 1.
24 Collins, 1953, p. 105.
25 Ibid., p. 99.

CHAPTER 3 *The Word Incarnate*

1 E. Hennecke, *New Testament Apocrypha*, volume 1, SCM, 1963.
2 Irenaeus, *Against Heresies*, III, ii, 8.
3 E.g., between the accounts of David's census in 2 Samuel 24 and the other version in 1 Chronicles 21.
4 From the Greek 'dia tessarōn'; i.e., one gospel 'through four'.
5 Origen, for example, carefully notes the discrepancies between John and the synoptics on the Temple cleansing and then denies historicity to *all* the accounts! In other instances of inconsistency, he explains that there is 'an admixture of that which is apparently unhistorical in order to exercise the intelligence.' See R. P. C. Hanson, *Allegory and Event*, SCM, 1959, p. 261ff.
6 For a concise reassessment of these methods, see G. B. Caird, 'The Study of the Gospels', *Expository Times*, Jan. Feb. and March 1976.
7 'Q' probably stands for the German Quelle, meaning 'source'. The Q theory is doubted by a significant minority of critical scholars.
8 See M. Dibelius, *From Tradition to Gospel*, James Clarke, 1935.
9 *The History of the Synoptic Tradition*, Basil Blackwell, 1963, p. 218ff., especially p. 239. Compare G. Vermes, *Jesus the Jew*, Collins, 1973, p. 69ff.
10 See N. Perrin, *What is Redaction Criticism?* SPCK, 1970.
11 See A. Schweitzer, *The Quest of the Historical Jesus*, A. & C. Black, 2nd edn., 1936; for more recent developments see H. K. McArthur, *In Search of the Historical Jesus*, SPCK, 1970.
12 See C. H. Dodd, *The Apostolic Preaching and its Development*, Hodder & Stoughton, 1963.
13 See Matthew 10:13 and Mark 11:21f.; and more generally J. M. Hull, *Hellenistic Magic and the Synoptic Tradition*, SCM, 1974.
14 J. D. G. Dunn, *Christology in the Making*, SCM, 1980, p. 264.
15 See E. Yamauchi, *Pre-Christian Gnosticism*, Tyndale Press, 1973.

16 Compare Sirach (Ecclesiasticus) 51:23—7; see further M. J. Suggs, *Wisdom, Christology and Law in Matthew's Gospel*, Harvard, 1970.

17 See C. F. Evans, 'Parable and Dogma' in *Explorations in Theology 2*, SCM, 1977, ch. 8.

18 C. H. Dodd, *The Parables of the Kingdom*, 1935, Fount, 1982, p. 13f.

19 See N. Perrin, *Rediscovering the Teaching of Jesus*, SCM, 1967 and W. G. Kümmel, *Promise and Fulfilment*, SCM, 1957.

20 N. Perrin, *Jesus and the Language of the Kingdom*, SCM, 1976, revises his earlier views (see above, n. 19) in the light of recent studies of the way parable functions linguistically. See also D. O. Via, *The Parables, their Literary and Existential Dimension*, Fortress Press, 1967, and J. D. Crossan, *In Parables*, Harper & Row, 1973.

21 E.g., M. D. Goulder, 'Characteristics of the Parables in Several Gospels' in *Journal of Theological Studies*, Oxford University Press, n.s. 19, 1968.

22 In particular, D. Cupitt, *Jesus and the Gospel of God*, Lutterworth, 1979.

23 Compare Matthew 10:33 and Luke 12:9; see recently J. Riches, *Jesus and the Transformation of Judaism*, DLT, 1980, p. 167, and A. E. Harvey, *Jesus and the Constraints of History*, Duckworth, 1982, p. 163.

24 See Daniel 2:44, but contrast Daniel 4:34.

25 See Matthew 16:13; compare Mark 8:27.

26 In accordance with contemporary Aramaic idiom, see G. Vermes, *Jesus the Jew*, Collins, 1973, p. 188ff.

27 E. Leech, *Genesis as Myth and Other Essays*, Jonathan Cape, 1969, p. 8.

28 See R. H. Fuller, *The Formation of the Resurrection Narratives*, SPCK, 1972.

29 See RSV notes at Mark 16:8.

30 As B. Lindars, *The Gospel of John*, New Century Bible, Oliphants, 1972, especially p. 51ff.

31 See R. E. Brown, *The Community of the Beloved Disciple*, Chapman, 1979.

32 J. Hick (ed.), *The Myth of God Incarnate*, SCM, 1977 and M. Goulder (ed.), *Incarnation and Myth, the Debate Continued*, SCM, 1979.

33 For a discussion of the difficulty, see C. K. Barrett, *Jesus and the Gospel Tradition*, SPCK, 1967.

34 R. E. Brown, K. P. Donfried and J. Reumann, *Peter in the New Testament*, Augsburg Paulist Presses, 1973, p. 86ff.

CHAPTER 4 *Believing in the Body of Christ*

1 Demetrius, *On Style*, sections 228 and 232.
2 See R. Bultmann, *Theology of the New Testament*, vol. 2, SCM, 1952; and contrast E. P. Sanders, *Paul and Palestinian Judaism*, SCM, 1977.
3 W. Marxsen, for example, *Introduction to the New Testament*, Basil Blackwell, 1968, p. 37ff.
4 On this see J. C. Hurd, Jr., *The Origin of 1 Corinthians*, SPCK, 1965.
5 M. D. Hooker, *Pauline Pieces*, Epworth, 1979, chapter 3.
6 See further C. K. Barrett, *The Signs of an Apostle*, Epworth, 1970.
7 C. F. D. Moule, *The Origin of Christology*, Cambridge University Press, 1977 connects Jesus' use of Son of Man with Paul's language of incorporation into Christ.
8 See E. Schweizer, *The Church as the Body of Christ*, SPCK, 1965.
9 J. L. Houlden, *Patterns of Faith*, SCM, 1977 appears to reach this conclusion.
10 Among recent commentators, J. L. Houlden, *Paul's Letters from Prison*, Penguin Books, 1970, p. 235ff., argues against authorship by Paul; G. B. Caird, *Paul's Letters from Prison*, Oxford University Press, 1976, p. 9ff., in favour.
11 C. K. Barrett, *The Pastoral Epistles*, Oxford University Press, 1963, p. 17f., notes the contribution of the pastorals towards the canonization of Paul; see also A. T. Hanson, *Studies in the Pastoral Epistles*, SPCK, 1968.
12 See G. Hughes, *Hebrews and Hermeneutics*, Cambridge University Press, 1979.
13 See *Early Christian Writings*, Penguin Books, 1979.
14 As H. Conzelmann, *The Theology of St Luke*, Faber, 1960; contrast S. G. Wilson, *The Gentiles and the Gentile Mission in Luke Acts*, Cambridge University Press, 1973, ch. 3.
15 Recent studies include E. Schweizer, *Luke, a Challenge to Present Theology*, SPCK, 1982, and N. Richardson, *The Panorama of Luke*, Epworth, 1982.
16 See further J. Jervell, *Luke and the People of God*, Augsburg, 1972.

CHAPTER 5 *A Biblical Agenda*

1 As examples of the approach needed here, see K. Stendahl, *The Bible and the Role of Women*, Fortress Press, 1966, and J. A. Baker, 'Racism and the Bible', in *Crucible*, December 1980.

2 See B. S. Childs, *Biblical Theology in Crisis*, Westminster Press, 1970.

3 See B. Smalley, *The Study of the Bible in the Middle Ages*, Basil Blackwell, 3rd edn., 1983.

4 W. M. Abbott (ed.), *The Documents of Vatican II*, Chapman, 1966, p. 127.

5 BRF, St Michael' House, 2 Elizabeth Street, London SW1; BRF, PO Box M, Winter Park, Florida 32790.

6 The formula is A. N. Whitehead's.

7 See H. R. Weber, *Experiments with Bible Study*, WCC, 1981, and W. Wink, *Transforming Bible Study*, SCM, 1981.

8 G. Cuming (ed.), *The Ministry of the Word*, BRF and Oxford University Press, 1979 may be used as an aid to this kind of corporate preparation for the liturgical reading of scripture.

9 See, e.g., R. H. Fuller, *The Use of the Bible in Preaching*, BRF, 1981.

10 See, e.g., J. Gelineau, *The Liturgy Today and Tomorrow*, DLT, 1978.

11 See The Doctrine Commission of the Church of England, *Believing in the Church*, SPCK, 1981, chapter 4.

12 B. R. Wilson, *Religion in Secular Society*, Penguin Books, 1969, p. 152.

13 At a press conference in Canada, 1981.

Index of Biblical References

OLD TESTAMENT AND APOCRYPHA

	Pages		Pages		Pages
Genesis		*Job*		*Daniel*	
1:3	45	19:25f	35f	2:44	109 n.24
4:10	107 n.2			4:34	109 n.24
15:6	71	*Psalms*		7:13f	33,56
29	5	2:7	31		
		45:6f	32	*Hosea*	
Exodus		47:7	31	13:11	31
3:14	27	74	107 n.12		
6:3	107 n. 14	110:1	31	*Amos*	
		147:16ft	45	8:11	102
Numbers				9:7	29
15:37—41	35	*Proverbs*			
		8:22,30	47	*Zechariah*	
Deuteronomy				9:9	32
6:4—5	49	*Isaiah*			
8:2,4	28	7:14	32	*Malachi*	
17:20	32	29:13	9	4:5	21
22:12	35	40:6,8	46		
		51:9—11	107 n.12	*2 Esdras*	
1 Samuel		53:7f	30	3—14	31
8	31	56:7	33		
		61:2	38	*Wisdom of Solomon*	
2 Samuel				7:25f	47
24	108 n.3	*Jeremiah*		9:10	47
		1:9f	45	18:16	47
1 Chronicles		23:7f	29		
21	108 n.3			*Ecclesiasticus* (Sirach)	
		Ezekiel		24:23	47
2 Chronicles		1:10	40	51:23—7	109 n.16
42:21	107 n.2	5:5	45		
				2 Maccabees	
Ezra				15:39	33
3:10—13	107 n.14				

	Pages		Pages		Pages
Matthew		19:41	57	*2 Corinthians*	
6:34	22n4	24:19f	34	3:17f	9
10:13	108 n.13			3:18	89
10:33	109 n.23	*John*		12:2–4	75
10:40	77	1:12f	51		
11:28–30	48	1:14	46, 61	*Galatians*	
16:13	109 n.25	1:17	46	3:16	71
16:16–18	65	1:29	101		
18:20	48	4:4–15	4f	*Ephesians*	
19:28	65	10:9	62	2:6	82
21:9	57	14:6, 25	62	2:20	81
23:35	107 n.2	17	64	4:15f	82
23:37–9	57	21	59		
24:43	54			*Philippians*	
25:6	54	*Acts*		3:8	92
28:19	46	8:34	30	3:20	79
		10:24ff	86		
Mark		15:7–11	86	*Colossians*	
2:26	63	15:28	60	1:18, 24	78
2:28	56	16:4	60	2:9	78
4:13–20	50f			3:3	78
4:41	61	*Romans*			
6:5	63	1–8	70, 72	*1 Thessalonians*	
6:56	35	1:3–4	43	1:10	43
7:8	9	1:16	72		
8:27	109 n.25	3:8	72	*2 Thessalonians*	
8:31	56	5	73	2:2	74
8:38	53	9–11	70, 72		
9:11	107 n.3	11:17f	28	*2 Timothy*	
10:5f	21			2:17f	82
11:21f	108 n.13	*1 Corinthians*		3:15f	23
12:1–9	21	1:12f	74		
13:7	54	3:11	81	*Philemon*	
13:24	56	6:15	78	10	68
13:31	55	7:1	68	20	76
14:7	107 n.4	9:20–2	71	22	68
16:8	109 n.29	10:4	94		
		10:16	78	*James*	
Luke		10:32ff	74	2:24	84
4:18f	39	11:26	58		
9:53	57	11:29, 33f	78	*2 Peter*	
10:30–7	52	12:4–11	8	3:13f	80
12:9	109 n.23	12:27	78		
17:20ff	54	13	13	*Revelation*	
19:38	57	13:12	89	4:6–8	40f
		15	72	7:17	34
		15:3–4	9, 43	21:6	34
				22:13	34
				22:18f	67

Index of Names and Subjects

Allegory 23,36,41,50,95
Angelus 49
Apocrypha, Old Testament 21
　　New Testament 40 &n.1
Augustine of Hippo 21,75

Barr, J. 18
Bible Reading Fellowship
　　93 & n.5
Bonhoeffer, D. 28f,37
Brown R. 19,103

Caird, G.B. 18
Canon of scripture 3,21f,39f,
　　69f,79f,91
Catholicism, free biblical 17f
Chalcedon, Council of 60,62
Christological reading of
　　scripture 30−4,94
Covenant Theology 24
Cranmer, Thomas 2
Creation 26−8
Critical method 2f,12−17,102

Dead Sea sect 22
Demetrius, On Style 69 n.1
Diatessaron 41
Dogmatic reading of
　　scripture 60−4

Ecumenism 11f,99f
Eschatology 8,22,51−5,65,85f

Ethics of the Bible 88f
Eucharist 39,59,95−8
Exodus 13,23,28f

Faith, as method 2f
　　and tradition 7−12
Form criticism of the
　　gospels 42
Franklin, E. 66

Gore, Charles 18
Gospel, oral 8f,38f,43
Gospels, plurality of 38−44
Gnosticism 22,47,63,65

Hebrews, letter to the 83f
Homilies, First Book of 2

Ignatius of Antioch 9,85
Incarnation, Old Testament
　　background 47
　　in the Synoptic
　　gospels 48,61
　　in the fourth gospel 61f
　　in Paul 76−9
Inspiration of scripture 7f,95

Jerome 21,92
John Chrysostom 95

Kingdom of God, in Jesus'
　　teaching 32,53f

Lectio divina, see Spiritual
   reading
Liturgy 9,13,55—9,95—8
Luther, Martin 10,75
Lux Mundi 18

Marcion 22
Messianism 31f, 34
Montreal, Faith and Order
   Conference 11f
Moule, C.F.D. 66
Myth 63

Name of God 14,27
Nicaea, Council of 9

Origen 106 n.6,108 n.5
Oxford Movement 17f,103

Paul, anthropology of 72f
   anti-paulinism of 73f
   Body of Christ in 76—9
   Justification by faith
  in 69f
   letters of 67—9,84
Parables of Jesus, 50—3

'Q' 41 & n.7,50

Redaction criticism of the
   gospels 42—4,61
Religion of Israel 24
Renewal of the Church 98—101
Resurrection of Jesus 13,59
Richards, H.J. 87
Robinson, J.A.T. 66

Sacramental nature of
   scripture 7,39,98
Salvation history 25
Sawyer, J. 37
Schmidt,W. 37
Secularization 99
Shaliach 77
Shema' 49
Sola scriptura 16f
Son of Man 33,53—6,77
Song of Songs 36f
Source criticism of the
   Pentateuch 4
      of the gospels 41
Spiritual reading of
   scripture 92—5
Stendahl, K. 87
Stolz, F. 37
Story, scripture as 13,28f,55—9
Suffering, problem of 28,
   33,55

Targum, Palestinian 6 & n.5
Tatian 40
Theology of the Bible 88,90f
Tradition 8—12
Trent, Council of 10,12

Vatican II, Council 11f,92

Wainwright, A.W. 19
Wesley, John 75
Whiteley, D.E. 87
Wijngaards, J.N.M. 103
Wilson, B.R. 99 n.12
Wisdom, Old Testament figure
   of 47
Word of God in the Old
   Testament 44—9